HAND-BUILT POTTERY
A Book for Schools and Students

PHOTO: FRS

Slab bottles: Mollie Winterburn.

HAND-BUILT POTTERY

A Book for Schools and Students

MOLLIE WINTERBURN

with sketches by the author

MILLS & BOON LIMITED, LONDON

First published 1966 by Mills & Boon Limited,
50 Grafton Way, Fitzroy Square, London W 1
© *Mollie Winterburn 1966*

Phototypeset by BAS Printers Limited, Wallop, Hampshire
and printed by Ebenezer Baylis & Son Limited,
The Trinity Press, Worcester and London

To my father, John Franklin Winterburn,
who would have been delighted

CONTENTS

ACKNOWLEDGEMENTS

May I make my sincere and grateful thanks to the many kind people who have helped me in the preparation of this book.

Firstly to my friend, Nora Gibbs, for somehow deciphering and typing my manuscript.

Secondly to generous people who have taken photographs for me, particularly Mr. F. R. Simmons who has done so many so well, also Mr. A. E. Hooton, Mr. W. D. White, Miss P. M. Matthews and Mr. Ted Bell; and to *The Daily Telegraph* for permission to reproduce a photograph. The individual photographs are identified in their places by initials.

Also to two of my colleagues, Roy Howarth and Tony Madgwick, for willing co-operation in projects; and to staffs of the various museums who have allowed me to make sketches.

Last, but certainly not least, to the many nice, keen and enthusiastic, helpful and hardworking children with whom I have worked.

PREFACE

The main purpose of this book is to be of use to teachers and children doing pottery in primary and secondary schools. So, rather than being a complete book of pottery making, it becomes almost a record of work, trying to describe suitable techniques and give ideas for people with only simple equipment, but who have lively interest and enthusiasm; and, while providing a sound basis of craftsmanship, to explore and experiment and be fully creative. All the work photographed has been done by my pupils or myself.

Any theories or opinions expressed in the book are my own and should not be taken as implicating my Local Education Authority.

M. W.

Chapter One

BEGINNING

Very many people who would like to teach pottery are discouraged from doing so because they feel there are so many difficulties and that it must have a special room and so much expensive equipment. Certainly it is much better to have a special place for clay work, but weak to tamely accept defeat for lack of one. All that is really necessary is determination —with enthusiasm—for much lovely pottery can be made with very little beyond what can be easily and cheaply obtained. So this book deals mainly with pottery which needs little or no apparatus, and work using wheels is only briefly mentioned. There the manipulation of the machine and tools are an obstacle and it is more satisfying to begin with direct contact with the clay.

I began to teach pottery myself with forty children in a class room with ordinary desks which was used for written English in the succeeding lesson. Clay we obtained either by digging for it ourselves or by asking for it at the coal mine where it was a waste product. Both needed cleaning; that from the pit having specks of coal in addition to the usual impurities. The enormous value of what must sound to be unnecessary labour is that there was no danger of the children thinking that clay was something which came in polythene bags! Very nice and convenient this is, of course— for when bought plastic and kept unopened in the polythene it will keep in good condition for a considerable time, so that storage is no great problem. Half hundredweights are convenient, for they are the biggest size which is easy to handle.

Almost the first thing these children had to learn was wedging and kneading. This again unintentionally turned out to be quite the best possible thing; firstly because all clay should be wedged before use, secondly because, like most schools, we had no pug mill, and keeping the clay in condition is always the worst problem one has to face. So much the easiest way of ensuring usable clay, is for every child to understand how to treat it and to be capable of wedging it up for themselves.

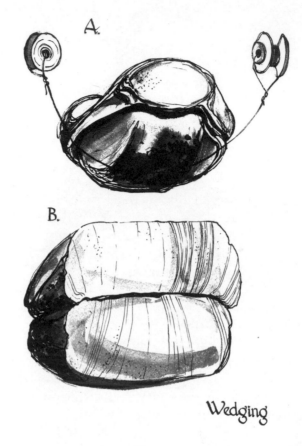

Wedging

Fig. 2

This I have found the easiest method to teach to children—

Tap the lump of clay into a shape longer than it is wide and let it fall to the table so that it makes an angle of about 40° with the table (Fig. 2) (A). Cut in two moving the wire upwards, lift and turn over the upper part and bring it down firmly on top of the other half so that the two cut edges lie one above the other facing the worker (B). Lift both and bring down so that the cut edges face away. Lift again and half turn to the right. Now, instead of bringing the clay down heavily, let one end fall so that it is in the first position again (A) ready for cutting a second time. Repeated between 20 and 30 times according to condition, this will disperse any harder or softer parts of the clay and make it of one consistency throughout and ready for use.

A good way to demonstrate this is to mix clay of different colours—the pattern of lines increasing in number and diminishing in size with each cut, until the clay is all of one colour, is easily seen.

C.

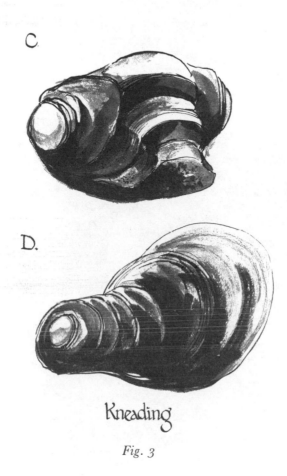

D.

Kneading

Fig. 3

Both wedging and kneading are far, far better seen than described—the latter being almost impossible in words! Diagram C (Fig. 3) shows the shape obtained by both hands working together from the edges pressing into the lump of clay, then lift forward—this is a circular movement. D shows a rotary movement with the weight of the shoulders coming down rhythmically on to the wrist, turning the clay clockwise, the hand taking a fresh hold after each. pressure and release. It is also possible to achieve the same result by foot pressure in a rotary movement—the effect of any of these methods being to move the clay on the outside towards the centre of the mass and slowly out again to the edge. This causes the flat clay particles to lie more parallel, thus increasing the plasticity.

Fig. 4   Mary's jug, coiled and painted.

Keeping clay damp without a good damp cupboard used to be almost a nightmare. Old dried-milk tins with pieces of brick and water in the bottom, consequent rust and whiskers of mould. Now there are polythene bags it is easy, and so long as there are no splits and they are kept airtight by tucking the end firmly underneath the board the pot will keep in a workable condition for weeks. If central heating makes conditions extraordinarily warm and dry, then a wet sponge or a piece of cloth can be put in with the pot. Even when one does have damp cupboards they never cater for more than 20% of the children so polythene bags are a "must".

On the contrary plaster must be kept quite dry, otherwise it "goes off" and will no longer set. For this reason it is better to buy it in large quantities. To get it by the hundredweight and have a bin with hundredweight capacity is ideal—seven-pound bags soon absorb damp from the atmosphere and become useless. Fine dental plaster is the best, and slow setting the most useful. The very quick setting plaster is good for waste moulding, for it chips off easily, but for pottery moulds the slow setting will be found to be harder and less easily broken.

Decidedly primitive kilns were built outside, one of the advantages of not having the grounds beautifully tidy and organised with lawns and flower beds, so that when we did eventually get a small electric kiln its use was thoroughly understood. It was not an incomprehensible gadget for turning clay into pottery but an alternative method of heating.

Slips and glazes, too, we made ourselves, frequently having failures but again the inestimable advantage of finding out, of experimenting, and of knowing one's materials—no one could be under the illusion that slips and glazes were things to be found in buckets.

There was, of course, the caretaker, quite and absolutely determined that there should be "No messing about with clay in HIS school". So we made him a mug. When our incompetence and inexperience blocked up the sink we made his wife a vase. When our electric kiln arrived and upset the entire school's electricity supply we made his grandson a horse. Needless to say he was really a very kind and patient man.

Ideally of course one would want a large room with a sink with a well, many strong benches (somehow there is never enough room), lots of damp cupboards and lots of storage bins, a pugmill, a really big kiln and a test kiln and space outdoors for kiln making, a clay supply in the vicinity, a banding wheel per child, and a small number of pupils! None of us has this, nor is it likely that we ever shall, so we all do the best we can with what we have.

The essential is the clay. Cutting wire is necessary for wedging. Wooden tools can be bought or shaped from odd pieces. Rolling pins and sponges are extremely useful and so are odd pieces of cloth. With these an enormous amount can be done. Places where various tools and apparatus can be obtained are listed at the back of the book.

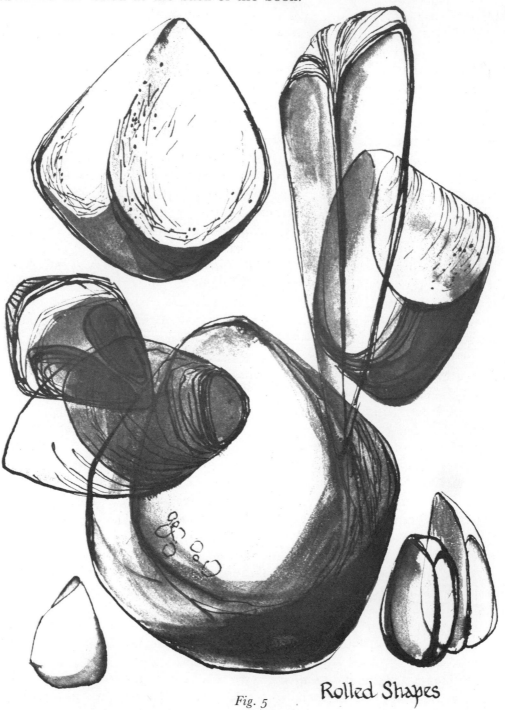

Fig. 5   Rolled Shapes

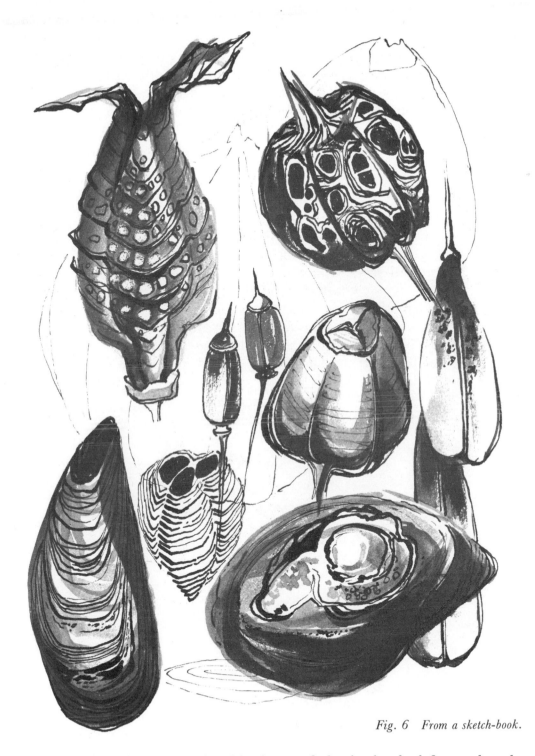

Fig. 6   From a sketch-book.

Most children like clay—should a lump of plastic clay be left on a bench,
I have rarely known a child, or an adult, enter the room without wanting

21

to touch it and leave the mark of their fingers on it. So first things to do might encourage feeling the material and exploring its possibilities, perhaps making a sphere, tapping one side flat to make a different plane and an asymmetric form, rolling one part to make a point, making a hollow, twisting and bending the shape, pulling part of it out, pressing one plane on to a textured surface, making a hole.

But this getting to know what clay will do is even better learnt with a purpose in mind. Exploration of the material ceases to be enjoyment if too long drawn out a process, for almost all children want to make something, to have the thrill of achievement, and more often than not it is a desire to make something useful. A shape found by rolling and tapping the clay, or a shape inspired by a pebble or seedcase, sometimes gives a thrill of appreciation—it would make a superb pot. But it must also be superbly made. If not it won't stand the test of firing. So good teaching of method is absolutely essential or disappointment and frustration are the result. One can find or stimulate ideas for forms, but without the basic knowledge of "how to do it" the ideas are never fulfilled and are irretrievably lost. But once the knowledge and the skill are there, there is no bar to achievement—one has been given the tools with which to create.

Chapter Two

PINCH POTTERY

Making a pinch pot is a very good way to start pottery making, for it is really starting to handle and feel the clay to see what it will do, to press it and pull it into shape, above all to sense when it is even in thickness. Not unexpectedly the oldest pottery that has been found was pinched out —just a lump of clay hollowed into a shape—which, after all, is an instinctive thing to do. The oldest pots made in England of which I know were tiny pinched out containers, which stood on a small pedestal also pinched to shape in clay, by the fire of prehistoric man, to dry out seawater to obtain rock salt—many thousands of years ago. Small hollowed out baked clay containers for fat, found in caves in South Western France, were also roughly pressed to shape and gave what must have been only a poor and flickering light by which prehistoric man produced the most superb drawings of animals deep inside the earth.

Making a pinch pot

Choose clay which is plastic, but not so soft that it will not be able to retain its shape and sag, and roll it into a ball. Roll it in the hands, not on the bench for that will give it ridges and angles, and it should be as near to a perfect sphere as possible. The size of the ball is important, for it should relate to the size of the hand. There is nothing more off-putting than too large a ball so that you do not feel able to control it completely. If it can be grasped comfortably then it is just right.

Hold it in the left hand—and it remains cupped in the left hand throughout the whole period of making. Make a hole in the ball by pressing in the right thumb—and check half way to see if you are steering straight. Try to leave the thickness at the bottom the final thickness that you intend for the whole pot—it is difficult to alter the base later on. I suggest a quarter of an inch for first attempts but thinner later.

Fig. 7   This pot was pinched into shape from local clay, dug and brought in by the children. The pattern was made by pressing in pebbles and the inside is glazed.

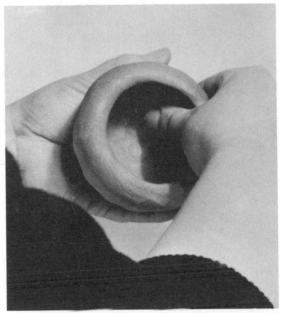

Fig. 8 Hands pinching

Then comes the actual pinching. Feel the thickness of the clay between the thumb (which is inside) and the fingers (which are outside) and squeeze gently. Turn the pot a little way round in the left hand and squeeze again, and so on right round the pot. Check that it is even; if one part seems thicker squeeze it more, all the time keeping the pot turning slowly and rhythmically in the left hand. It is this sensitivity to the feel of the clay which is the special value of making a pinch pot, this getting it firm and even which will make for good firing with no cracks or distortions. When satisfied move the thumb and fingers a little higher up and squeeze again, turning the pot slowly round as before. It is important to begin at the base and work upwards, for as the pot grows it is no longer possible to get fingers and thumb to the bottom. You have to decide at an early stage whether to leave in the ridges of the finger pressing, which can be both satisfying and decorative, or whether to pinch them out as you turn the

25

pot round and round to make a perfectly smooth finish. As you get to the top remember never to pinch the actual rim, for this will make a sharp edge, unsuitable, unattractive and liable to split.

If a long time is taken in making, the clay may dry out with the heat of the hands and begin to crack at the rim. Should this happen, rather than try to join them, it is better to be patient and stop altogether for a few minutes. Turn the pot rim down on to a damp cloth which will damp it evenly and where it needs it most, and in a short time it will be ready to continue working. Even if this treatment is not necessary it is always important to put the pot down on its rim, for put down on its base it would lose the curve because its own weight would cause it to spread out and the pot would sag and become heavy-looking. By the time it is complete it will have dried sufficiently with working to keep its shape when right way up, and with a gentle tap it will have a tiny flat area on which to stand yet retain the nice springing curve upwards that these pots, well made, always have. Should a pot have a tendency to wobble it can be cured by making a concave hollow in the middle of its base.

With practice it is possible to gain control over the shape, to make it long and slender or to keep it turned in at the rim. You might want to tap it into a squarish round or to almost a triangle.

If they have been polished and smoke blackened by firing in a sawdust kiln these pots look superb. Anything smooth can be used for polishing— a stone or a spoon will do—but wait until it is leather-hard. A contrast of rough and polished surfaces is most attractive, so too is a simple pattern round the form made by pressing in stones when it is soft and polishing as it becomes harder.

Joining

A frequent criticism of pinch pots is "They're so small", or "You can't make anything useful." What nonsense! If size is the only objection—and certainly at first, and even later to a large extent, it is governed by the size of the hand—then the obvious thing to do is to make a large pot by joining several together. Make two with the same diameter of rim, though in other respects they need not be the same size or shape, and invert one and join the two rims together. Cut a hole in what was originally the base of the upper one and either neaten it into a rim or join a third pot right way up, cutting through its base where it joins. Infinite variation of shape is possible in this way.

Simple Joinings

Fig. 9

It is also possible to make the pot larger by adding coils. Primitive potters of Ancient America and even nowadays in many parts of Africa, make superb pots on a pinched base by supporting the base in a rounded biscuited mould or on broken sherds while the rest of the pot is coiled. This ensures not losing the lovely rounded base which is so much more useful in a pot which has to stand on the ground.

Rolling

It is a favourite occupation of many of the children I teach to join two pinchpots rim to rim as above but instead of cutting a hole immediately, roll the shape on the bench. Results are rarely as preconceived and often very nice. The air inside ensures that it won't fold up; it can change its shape but not alter its volume. Beautiful rounded forms appear, or soft ridges might be made by rocking or rolling in different directions and these give varied planes and sometimes help to strengthen the form. These "stones" are lovely in themselves and are frequently kept like that to stand in groups. Parts of the surface can be enriched by texture, colour or glaze. Sculptural forms can be made by joining them together. They might be used as parts for mobiles.

Fig. 10   Valerie's "stones".

But do not forget to make a hole before they are fired, just a pinprick will do, as otherwise each one is a large air hole!

Fig. 11   Lidded pinch pots, first efforts in pottery making by eleven-year-olds.

Lidded pots

Another attractive thing which can be done with these rolled shapes is to make them into pots with lids. Flatten a part of the surface as a base, with a concave hollow if necessary, and let it become leather-hard. Then using the shape to best advantage and with any sharp tool cut out a lid. Not a straight cut at right angles to the wall of the pot, or the lid will just skid off, but at about 45° pointing down so that the lid sits into a hollow. It must not be so steep that it will leave too thin an edge. The sharpness of the cut must be rounded gently but very carefully so as not to take off too much or distort it so that the lid is no longer an exact fit. A knob must be made for lifting—a simple related shape or an opportunity to add a small lively piece of modelling.

29

Fig. 12   Cactus garden: Mollie Winterburn.

Cactus gardens

There is, of course, no need to join pinched shapes only one above another or rim to rim. They can be joined side by side, joined into sides at different heights, turned to different angles. There are infinite possibilities of grouping and of using light and shadow. A cactus garden is only one of many possible uses. Just one word of warning—care must be taken so that weight is well distributed and no one part has overhanging weight which may cause cracks in drying or firing. Also that different thicknesses are not joined together so that shrinkage is greater in one part than another, for this too will cause cracks. A combination of coiling with pinching is ideal for this kind of pot.

Whistles

When country potteries were much more common the young apprentices were allowed to make penny whistles a few weeks before Christmas to earn themselves some pocket money. The principle is simple—blow through a narrow aperture on to a sharp edge into an enclosed space with a small outlet hole. Once you've got it, it's so easy and always works. This is the way I find best.

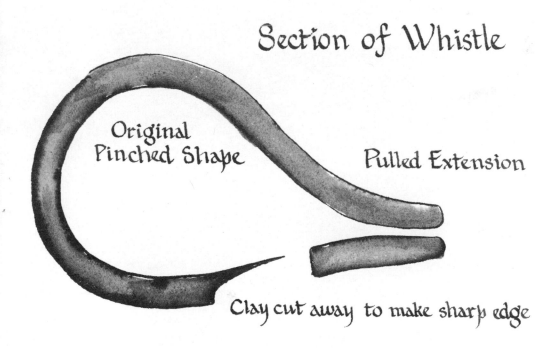

Section of Whistle

Original Pinched Shape

Pulled Extension

Clay cut away to make sharp edge

Make a pinch pot with only a tiny top opening. Press from the outside until this closes. Pull the solid lump it makes outwards, so elongating it. This is the part through which you blow. Next insert a small tool into the pot where this part joins and turn it to make a round hole. Now put the tool lengthways through the elongated part, heading towards the hole, until you can see it through the hole and see where it touches at the farthest side. This is the place to make into the sharp edge, so cut a semi-circular depression above it to make it thin. It will then whistle. If it really doesn't then you've done something wrong, so try again and don't be misled into thinking "Not to worry—it will whistle when it's fired". It won't. You make it whistle while it's still clay. Weird and wonderful is the sound when an entire class make whistles.

PHOTO: FRS

Fig. 14   Whistles, by Marilyn and the author.

You will gradually find out how size and shape alter the note and the tone. Without affecting this all kinds of modelling can be added; birds and fish are easy and popular, but one of my favourites was a reclining cow.

32

Panamanian Bird Whistle.

Fig. 15   By courtesy of the British Museum.

Some of the most wonderful whistles ever made were modelled by potters of Ancient America a thousand and more years ago. The British Museum has a splendid collection of these—there are birds, bears, dogs, monkeys, from Peru and the Andean zone to those from Bolivia, from Mexico and Panama and the Caribbean region. Many, like this one drawn in the Museum, have extra holes going directly into the form, and by covering these different notes can be produced. Most of the whistles are made in buff clay—they are not glazed but are polished and have painted patterns.

Japanese tea bowls

These bowls, used for the tea ceremony, were frequently also pressed and pinched to shape in the hands. They are filled from a ladle and passed round to the guests. As they have no handles it is a good thing they are fairly thick, so not too hot to hold in the hands. The raku glaze matures at a temperature of about 750°C, which is the red heat of a bonfire. It is great fun to have a raku firing with pinch pots, to see the glaze melt and take out the pots with a pair of long-handled tongs and drop them into a bowl of cold water. There is a loud hiss and almost at once the pots are ready to handle—they are passed round and excitedly discussed.

Chapter Three

COILING

It is a good idea to go from the very small to the very large. Pinch pots are usually quite tiny, coil pots are usually quite large. In fact it is much more difficult to make a really good small coil pot than it is to make a really big one. And coiling is one of the loveliest things to do—it is quiet, calm and peaceful; there comes a pleasant rhythm in working; the growth of the pot is seen and felt, but it grows slowly. It grows so slowly you can feel the development of its planes and its curves and have complete control over it. It needs practice before this rhythm and control come, but when they do most people enjoy the steady growth, the exploration of form and the fulfilment of building a pot with coils.

Pots like the large Cretan storage jars in Fig. 16 were made by coiling. The pots themselves have been coiled and the surface smoothed. On the finished surface more coils have been added for decoration—coils placed horizontally, occasionally vertically, sometimes criss-cross and frequently in waves. These have been pressed on, usually impressed with a pattern which serves the double purpose of decoration and helping to join the coil more firmly to the body of the pot.

Clay

It is much easier to make coil pots with an open groggy clay, so before beginning the actual shape make a suitable clay body by adding sand and grog as the clay is wedged. You will find this fairly rough clay very pleasant to handle. Experience and personal preference will decide the amount to be added—personally I slice the clay thinly and just sprinkle each slice with alternate sand and grog. Note the amount in comparison with the weight of clay—to know the proportion is important in case insufficient is wedged to complete the pot. It is better, of course, to make enough the first time, for it is very frustrating to have to stop for re-wedging just when really absorbed in the form.

Cretan Storage Jars

Fig. 16

Method

Coiling is done differently by different people and however or by whom taught somehow one drifts into one's own personal way of doing it, which, perhaps ever so slightly, differs from everyone else's. Basically all methods are the same in that a shape is built up from coils of clay joined together. Some people's coils are round, some are flat—intentionally so; some are almost the thickness of the finished pot in diameter while others are as much as three times that thickness and are pressed thinner after they are joined; some are joined above one another, some inside and some outside the growing pot; some are joined on the inside first, some the outside, and some not at all on one side; some are joined after each circumference and some spiral upwards the length of the coil; some coils are rolled on a flat surface, some coiled in the hand and hanging downwards. I was lucky, for I was first taught to coil by Helen Pincombe whose coiling is superb, yet the immense value I gained was not so much in the actual method as in the love of making—the calm rhythm and gradual growth of the form, and that is the most important thing, for one's own method just comes.

I have now many times had the experience of teaching a class, both children and adults, to coil, the entire class the same method; yet a few weeks later there will be several slight variations. If successful they are ignored—these people have become quite absorbed and developed their own method of working and it is good. Only when there are failures is it essential to find out why, perhaps to begin again.

Make a ball of clay for the base, pat it flat with the side of the hand down on to the board or banding wheel where the work is to be done. Leave it fairly thick—coil pots are mostly large—I would suggest half an inch, especially as it may be necessary to make a slight concave hollow later on to make the pot stand better.

Then begin to make coils. I take a lump of clay and press it roughly into a thick rope, turning it as I do, so that all indentations are not above one another. Place this on a flat surface (to which it will not stick—wood is ideal) and roll. Make it a real roll—not just over and back or it will not be round. Keep the fingers straight, the hands parallel with the table, and do not press too hard. Start at the middle and work outwards. I make these slightly over half an inch in diameter and use them for pots three feet in height. The general rule is, if anything make the coils thicker than necessary rather than thinner, for nothing is more difficult to deal with than a too thin wobbly pot. Besides this, as the pot is built it is easy to make

Fig. 17   Beryl's first coil pot. Height 16 inches. Painted in cobalt and iron.

the walls thinner but very difficult to make them thicker. Length of coil is not important, for they can be either joined or cut shorter; nevertheless aim for length. It is exasperating to have to constantly interrupt the movement of putting on a coil to make frequent joins because of short lengths. The only limit should be availability of space for rolling—in a classroom often a problem. It's tremendously important to make a large stock of coils before starting to put them on—again it is the interruption of the rhythm of working caused by stopping to make more coils. Personally, I make about a dozen at a time, approximately a yard long. Working space makes greater lengths impossible, and in number this builds up as great a height of pot as desirable at one go to avoid any danger of sagging—it is good to have a pause to make more coils while the pot dries slightly.

Fig. 18 Rolling coils.

Fig. 19 Jennifer coiling.

To put them on, hold one end up in the left hand, the other in the right. This latter end is put on the edge of the base and firmly joined with the thumb. Continue along the coil, pressing it down and on to the base on the inside with the right thumb. Note particularly that the coil is not put on and then thumbed down, but goes on as it is pressed down. This is important. If you doubt it try one both ways—the one put on before pressing will be found to be considerably longer—that is why many people find that pots tend to sag outwards. Break the coil when it gets to the starting point and join well. Then thumb down outside; in each case clay is actually pulled down from the coil on to the pot, as it is with succeeding coils. Second and successive coils are added in the same way; taking care not to put the joins above one another, for this would make a weak place in the pot. After every two or three coils go round the pot with thumb inside and fingers outside, pressing gently as in a pinch pot to steady and neaten the form. Shaping is done mainly by the placing of the coils—on top of one another or slightly to the outside or inside. Tapping with a flat piece of wood is a great help in strengthening and shaping the form— "If it doesn't do what you want, hit it", I overheard. Possession of a banding wheel is a great help, in fact makes coiling much easier, the wheel spinning gently clockwise as the coil is pressed on, a pause for joining, and anti clockwise as the outside is thumbed down, a pause as a new coil is picked up, and so on with a constant smooth flow until a new supply of coils is needed. Banding wheels are rather expensive but will easily last a lifetime.

Should the coils not have been of even thickness or the pot asymmetric it may be difficult to keep the top level. Hold something sharp against the lowest part and turn the pot so that a mark is made at this level all round —then cut.

Some people are content to leave the outside of coil pots with the corrugated effect of the unjoined coils. This is decorative and variations can be used in places of joining or thickness of coils. It is also less safe and could end up as a set of bracelets. To leave on the marks of the thumbs pressing down successive coils, perhaps all over, perhaps alternately or in groups or spaces, is also a way of using the method as decoration. However, it is not practical in use, and it is highly significant that peoples of early civilizations who had no other choice than coiled pottery for daily use found it advantageous to make their pots as smooth as possible to the extent of polishing with a stone.

It is hardly necessary to state that coil pots need not be round. The value of coils in asymmetric building is one of its greatest assets and keenest joys.

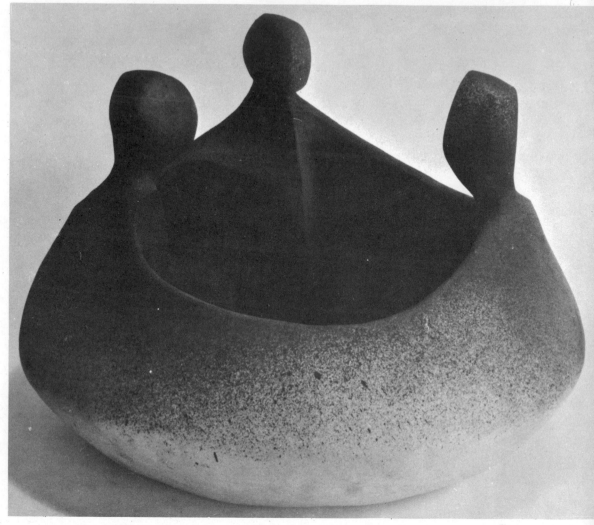

Fig. 20   "Conference": Mollie Winterburn.

British Neolithic

The earliest pots known were made by the first people ever to have a settled home, that is people of the New Stone Age. People before this had to be nomads, for they lived by hunting, fishing and gathering. The Neolithic discoveries of agriculture and the domestication of animals meant that people would choose a site suitable for agriculture and stay there for a considerable length of time. With the growth of settled communities crafts like pottery and weaving could be developed. Since some very early pottery has marks resembling woven baskets impressed on the outside there is a popular theory that the discovery of pottery was by baskets lined with clay being accidentally burnt. Certainly marks resembling baskets, or twisted thread or reed where it would have been used for carrying, were used for decoration over a long period. Yet the earliest known pottery in Europe which was made by the Danubian peoples (who later produced the spiral-meander pottery) had no decoration and is of a simple scoop shape like the cup made by a hand if one wants a drink and there is no receptacle available.

1700-1800BC.

c.1700BC.

Prehistoric British Pottery

Fig. 21   By courtesy of the Guildhall Museum.

The two jars in Fig. 21 were sketched in the Guildhall Museum and were both made between 1800 and 1700 B.C. They are quite lovely. They were coiled and smoothed, and the impressed and punctured decoration so obviously added for the satisfaction and delight of the potter.

43

Chinese Neolithic c. 2500 B.C.

Fig. 22   By courtesy of the Victoria and Albert Museum.

Chinese pottery is probably the most famous in the world and there are special discoveries in technique, and excellencies of form and pattern, relating to almost every period. The earliest known is the one I like best— the Neolithic pottery made between 5000 and 2000 B.C. in the north west of China. There was no shortage of clay—it has been said with justification that people lived in clay houses, with clay furnaces, surrounded by clay walls, and that their fields were soft with clay. Some of the best early pottery comes from the province of Kansu. Just as the first farmers in Europe chose to settle on loess uplands in the vicinity of water courses, and that is where the earliest pottery in Europe is found, so the land of Kansu was also loess highlands, plentiful in good pottery clay. Although much of the early Chinese pottery consists of bowls, jars and beakers which are plain and essentially utilitarian, some are superbly modelled shapes, small at the base and swelling to a round, full, vigorous, strong form. There are good examples of these in the Victoria and Albert Museum and all are coiled. They are buff in colour decorated with decisive lines of red and black in wide sweeping curves which emphasise and swing round the satisfying fullness of form.

Egyptian

The superb jar in Fig. 23, now in the Victoria and Albert Museum, was made nearly 6000 years ago in Egypt in pre-Dynastic times. It is earthenware, coiled and polished and nearly two feet high. Intended to stand in the sand, it has a small base and rises to a tall full form which has a lovely simplicity and dignity. Like others of the same period it is black at the lip and red at the foot, showing that it was fired inverted in an open fire, probably one of several half inside one another, the tops being blackened by the carbonisation of the dried grass on which they rested.

Pueblo—6th to 9th Century A.D.

Since in all Ancient America the wheel was not used, and until the Spanish conquest possibly unknown, all pottery was made entirely by hand. The three techniques used were (a) coiling, (b) a kind of pinching, hollowing out the centre and thinning the sides, and (c) moulding, this being the commonest. Much of the coiling, which resulted in superbly thin and beautifully rounded pots, was made with flattened coils placed a third of the way inside one another and usually being built up spirally.

These people were expert too in making suitable clay bodies for hand building. Besides crushed pottery they added such things as fragments of shell, mica, and volcanic ash to their clay. Decoration was with slips in an astonishingly large number of colours and the work was finished by polishing with smooth stones.

Pre-Dynastic Egyptian Jar

Fig. 23   By courtesy of the Victoria and Albert Museum.

Coiling as a method of sculpture

Almost without one's realising it a coiled pot can become a piece of sculpture. In any case it is an excellent method of modelling and quite the best for any large piece which has to stand firing.

Photo: frs

Fig. 24   Elaine's horse and rider.

The illustration in Fig. 24 is a model made by a child and is 16 inches high. Apart from the animal's legs, which are thin and therefore could be left solid, every other part of the building was done by coiling. This meant that to a certain extent the work had to be preconceived, but it was considerably simplified during making. Support was necessary under the horse's middle so that the weight was not on the legs during the making and this would be necessary for any part of a big model which overhangs a space. Internal support is often found necessary when coils meet over a space, and for this newspaper is excellent. It can be screwed and twisted into shape to fill any space and can be damped if necessary to help stop the work drying out too quickly. There were five copies of *The Times* inside one of the birds shown in Chapter Thirteen! But better not to forget to take it out, though a little in an inaccessible corner will burn out without doing any damage.

Advantages of the method

Not only is coiling a lovely thing to do, it also has certain very definite advantages over other methods of pottery making. Three I especially value.

Firstly, size. Very large pots and models can be made, in fact the method is particularly suited to a large scale and it is easier to make a large than a small coil pot. The limitation is the size of kiln. In the school where I teach there is a certain stick cut to size—the "height of kiln stick". How often it has been held against a pot with a sigh—when it dries will it shrink another inch and just go in?

The second special value is in use with other handbuilt methods. Very frequently a mixture of method is desirable and coiling is the easiest to combine, being the most adaptable and fitting most easily on to other shapes.

Thirdly and lastly, and of major importance, unlike the limitation imposed by the use of the wheel, a coil pot need not be round. It can be, of course, and near round is the easiest to do, but for the sheer joy of building up a sculptural form, balancing flat and curved surfaces, and having steady and complete control during working, coiling cannot be beaten.

PHOTO: TB

Fig. 25   Asymmetric pots by fifteen-year-olds. Cecilia's flower-holder is entirely coiled; the lamp bases by Carole and Christine include slabs.

Chapter Four

TILES AND MOSAICS

This is not so drab as it sounds! Not all tiles are square and flat or alike in pattern—though perfectly flat even square tiles certainly have their uses. Ceramic roof tiles and chimney pots have never been surpassed, though, as with floors, many other materials are used. Ceramic floor tiles are attractive and easy to clean but wear comparatively quickly and are cold; but they are still widely used in hearths. Flat tiles have become very popular for coffee table tops—as the complete surface or odd ones inset. If, for this, decoration with paint and glazes should be the only object, then many people buy commercially produced unglazed tiles, which are ideal—light and even and unlikely to shrink any more. Beware of glazed ones; unless you know the composition of the glaze underneath you may get a surprise.

Making flat tiles

There are many ways of making tiles, the very simplest being just to roll out clay on a board—sanded, so that it will not stick and crack in drying —to the correct thickness; and cut to size and shape. Some people use two battens screwed to the board to get the depth even. Some cut the clay in slices with wire from a well wedged block of clay.

With these methods two major difficulties become apparent at once. The first is a tendency to warp as the clay dries, but this is normally easy to deal with either by turning the tiles over as they dry or by scoring (cutting grooves) on the under side.

The second is much more serious, that is shrinkage. Though one knows it will normally be about one in ten using plastic clay, owing to the kind and its state it can vary enormously, so that it is difficult to calculate a final size. Also, unless all the tiles of a set are made at exactly the same time from exactly the same clay they may not even shrink to the same size as each other.

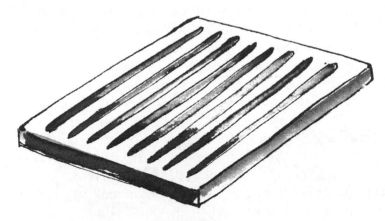

Scoring on the under side of a tile·

Fig. 26

Two other methods of making are to have either a plaster tile mould or a wooden tile box into which clay can be pressed—these have respectively a removable top or base so the tiles can be taken out at once for drying and the boxes reused. But these methods have the same two major problems, and if one really wanted to make so many flat tiles that it was worth the expenditure of buying a tile press then that is the best thing to do, for these have sufficient weight to press nearly dry clay so there is practically no shrinkage or warping. However, children I have taught made a successful chess table without a tile press, tiles being cut 4-in. square, and finally alternately glazed with a matt black glaze, and painted in cobalt and iron with a matt white glaze. Chessmen, of course, matched.

Medieval floor tiles
Tiles have been in use as flooring in English churches since the twelfth century. Previously floors were laid in slabs and blocks of differently coloured stone, and tiles, too, began by pattern-making using clay tiles of varied colours, shapes and sizes.

After this came patterned tiles, and during the finest period from the thirteenth to fifteenth centuries, there were intricate impressed tiles made both in one clay and with clay of a second colour, usually red clay with white inlaid. Glaze was used, the colours being yellow, green and black with, owing to impurities in the chemicals used, infinite variations. Size too varied, shrinkage seems to have been uncertain. Patterns were of infinite variety, geometric or floral, with animals or figures, with heraldry or with inscriptions. One complete thirteenth-century pavement still *in situ* is that of the Chapter House at Westminster.

The work was almost invariably of local origin; for example, while the monastery at Malvern was being built the local clay was used and a kiln erected on the spot. Work produced varied in quality, some being highly finished both in workmanship and design, but all, like medieval pottery in general, had liveliness and vigour. For making encaustic tiles it was necessary to have a bed of pipe clay in the neighbourhood. The tiles were made of secondary clay, firing red, and the design filled in with white pipe clay (so called because it was used for making clay pipes). These tiles were made in a wooden mould (tile box), usually square, and impressed with a carved wooden block. When almost leather hard the hollows were filled with white slip, then the top scraped level. The tiles were dried and before firing sprinkled with lead ore (raw glazing). The galena turned the white yellowish and made the red a richer colour. As a rule plain white tiles were obtained by slipping and plain black ones by colouring with manganese.

Sometimes these tiles were complete in themselves, sometimes a tile was a unit of a pattern, and sometimes several tiles made up one unit which was repeated or counterchanged with another. Some were specifically designed as borders having a starting and finishing tile, the intermediate pattern being repeated as often as required.

The Chertsey tiles are the most famous, and those used in Westminster Abbey, made about 1253–9, show the Confessor giving his ring to St. John, portraits of Henry III and his wife Eleanor, Archbishop Crokesley, the king on horseback with his dog, a hound and stag, the Royal Arms, and a border of St. Peter's salmon. Also produced at Chertsey was a series showing legends of Richard Coeur de Lion. Many museums have this kind of tile, and, besides those at Westminster, there are several still *in situ* in churches in various parts of the country, in Rievaulx Abbey, in Romney, Lewes, Winchester, Gloucester and many others.

There was another kind of tile produced at that time of which there are only a few surviving examples. That is where the tile was made of secondary clay, covered with white slip, and the slip then incised and cut away to leave raised white figures on a red ground. Of course they had to be made individually and so were, even then, less common.

Mediæval Encaustic Tiles
sketched at Tintern.

Fig. 27

In the fifteenth century there was a return to stone and marble for flooring, for sometimes tiles laid over a large area had become uneven or worn. However, it is significant that encaustic tiles keep their pattern longer than others because instead of being a surface pattern it is deeply inlaid.

Islamic tiles

In Islamic countries tiles with raised decoration were also made from moulds from the thirteenth century onwards. Again slip was used but these were decorated in many other ways too, particularly in painting, and notably in painting with lustre. Sometimes this painting was done under, sometimes over the glaze, rich blue and turquoise being favourite glaze colours. Decorated tilework actually plays a very important part in Islamic architecture. Mihrabs are architectural compositions inset into walls inside shrines and mosques to indicate the direction worshippers must face for prayer. These were mostly made of richly decorated tiles.

Kashan pottery is so famous for its tiles that the word Kashi has become a common word for tile. For over a hundred years, *c.* 1200–1300, most of these tiles were made by members of one family and are signed and dated. These tiles were painted in lustre and sometimes had relief modelling added, or rich glaze to pick out inscriptions—for Persian verses, moralising or amorous, were used as decoration just as were figures, human and animal. Many of these superb wall tiles were made in interlocking star and cross shapes.

Egyptian tiles

Tiles had been in use in Egypt many centuries previously. Some low relief ones from the temple at Abydos (First Dynasty) are interesting in that they have a dovetailed tenon at the back through which holes have been drilled to assist in securing the tile. Sometimes these would be used to decorate the jamb of a doorway as in the pyramid at Saqqara. Fragments of superbly painted Egyptian tiles can be seen in many museums, so that one gets tantalising glimpses of the wonderful animal and bird painting at which they excelled. Effects of lighting may have been unusual, for many of these tiles had a slightly convex face.

Tiles of many other countries are of great beauty and interest and make good subjects of study, such as tiles from Syria and Turkey, Hispano–Moresque tiles, those from India and China (roof tiles), Germany (stove tiles) and Delft.

Making a tile panel

The most fascinating and exciting tiles to make are tiles for pictures. These have no need of a flat surface, no need to be of equal thickness all over, no need to be symmetrical and certainly no need to be like one another. There is absolutely endless scope for experiment in textures, also in colours and in glazing, in use of light and shadow with low relief, in contrast of glazed and unglazed surfaces, and, of course, in subject matter too. Any kind of clay can be used from a smooth to a very coarse mixture. Sizes can vary from very tiny to the largest the kiln will hold; indeed this variation and contrast of size of piece is one of the most attractive features and can be used to great advantage.

PHOTO: PMM

Fig. 28   "Buttercup"—Janet's first tile picture.

My normal method is to roll out the clay on a slightly sanded board to about ¼-in. in thickness. Then I sketch on the design very roughly, using anything that makes an indentation, usually a porcupine quill, and immediately begin to build up the design in low relief using the spare clay cut from the edges, putting it on in balls or in coils, modelling with it, scratching it, making impressions in it—all of which serve the double purpose of making an interesting texture and joining the added clay firmly to the foundation. For impressions I use sticks and pebbles, fruit stones and nuts, cones and seedpods and seed cases, bark and shells; anything else which comes to hand such as a piece of old broom, an elderly dishcloth,

55

a piece of chain—though always the inimitable asymmetric shape of the natural object is more attractive. Sometimes textures might be gently rolled; perhaps then added to.

Photo: PMM

Fig. 29   Marks made in clay.

When complete, and having due regard to the design, the panel is cut, some pieces large and some tiny; and when leather-hard, edges are neatened. This slight smoothing, which inevitably takes a little off, is quite deliberate, for it allows for the slight unevenness in shrinkage which one gets in this method owing to the different thicknesses in the clay. Next comes painting; some areas are coloured and some left, in some it is painted into the pattern, in others dry brushed over the top to leave hollows which might later be filled with glaze. Sometimes paint may be scraped from the surface leaving a texture inlaid in colour; scratching into the colour is also effective. Allow a good long drying time because some parts will be quite thick.

After biscuit firing it may be all or partly glazed. Finally with a really good strong adhesive it is joined to its base and the narrow gaps between the pieces grouted with plaster—this often adds very advantageously to the decorative effect. One word of warning—if not to be mounted directly into position, don't use too heavy a base or the wall will not take the weight!

There is, of course, no necessity for the ceramic pieces to cover all the base. Individually built up tile pieces leaving spaces big or small can be used. The plaster or cement can be left plain, it can be textured, it can be painted into, before it sets weeds and leaves can be pressed into it and removed, things like pebbles, sticks, shells and string can be pressed in and thinly covered and left. String is very useful—thick string and thin string, smooth string and hairy string.

PHOTO: PMM

Fig. 30   Fish panel with pebbles set in plaster.

As well as being done individually these tile panels make an excellent project for a group of people—in which case the value of allowing for background instead of fitting the pieces exactly together is immediately apparent. A group of young children I taught once chose the "Pied Piper". Rats for models were borrowed from the animal house and the variety in results was startling. It is quite a good idea to use colour limitation as a method of keeping a unity in panels composed by several people.

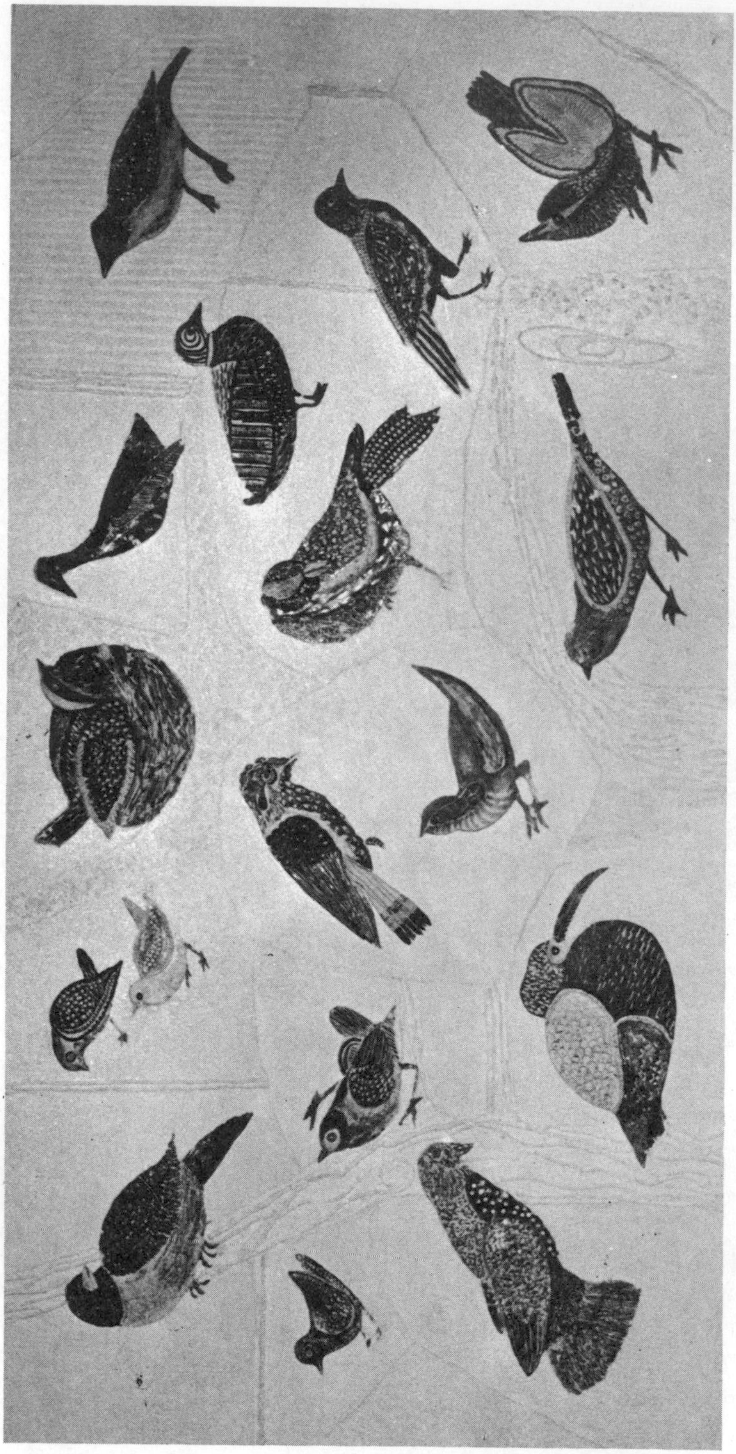

Fig. 31 Bird panel made by 2H.

58

Fig. 33   Detail from large bird panel.

These naturally are far from being the only decorative methods. I have not mentioned textures from glazes or carved and incised patterns, nor specifically using different heights of pieces in the planning of light and shadow—this can be done either by actually different thicknesses or setting at different levels.

Tile panel making is a lovely thing to do, lively and inventive, and creative at every stage of the work.

Fig. 32   Detail from large bird panel showing use of string, stones and scratching in the plaster.

Figs. 31, 32 and 33 show a panel done by a group of twelve-year-olds. Each child made a bird, but after weeks of looking at birds and drawing birds, getting information from books and visiting the Natural History Museum. Colouring was limited to iron and manganese. It is eight feet by four feet high. Sections were planned and each section separately walled off with clay and filled in with plaster. Some are plain, some textured with a plaster tool or cockscomb, some have stones put in and some match sticks. String has been used a great deal; some of it was dipped into plaster first, then pressed on to the just-setting background.

Mosaics

In many early cultural periods small carvings in wood, ivory or stone sometimes had tiny pieces of stone or enamel inserted. In particular this is seen in Egypt, where amazingly skilful techniques in using glass were also introduced. Mosaics grew when the area inlaid exceeded that of the original material, so that instead of a decorated carving the base became a background or a frame. The pieces are called tesserae. Mosaics have been widely used as floor and wall coverings.

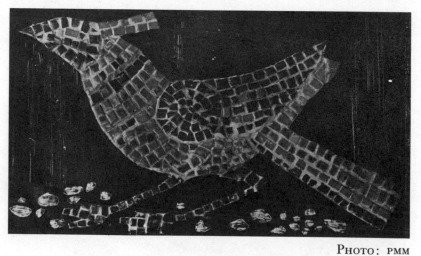

PHOTO: PMM

Fig. 34   Child's mosaic.

Roman floors

One of the most striking features of ancient Rome was the use of mosaic for pavements, and many of these have proved astonishingly durable. Mosaics are not necessarily of one material, though apparently some of the earliest in Rome were made entirely of marble; some are made of black and white marble and red tile, some use glass and some semi-precious stones. Ceramic tesserae supply many lovely earth colours which were widely used—reds, buffs and browns. Subjects include geometric patterns, birds and flowers, horsemen, charioteers, fish, vases, and signs of the zodiac.

Their use naturally spread to all countries of the Roman Empire, and remains of many beautiful floors of Roman villas have been found and can still be seen in various parts of England—in Lullingstone, Colchester, York, Dorchester and Bignor, St. Albans and very many other places.

The ancient Roman method was to cover the hypocausts (heating systems) with large tiles resting on bricks, upon these a layer of smaller bricks set herring-bone style with a thin stratum of lime and chalk cement superimposed, and upon this were fixed the tesserae.

Walls in Ravenna

Of course the very special place to see Byzantine mosaics is Ravenna and there they are seen at their best. The flatness of architectural forms in the sixth century gave enormous scope for decoration on walls in churches, as in S. Apollinare Nuovo, where there is a simple straight row of saints which is so fitted to the wall that it seems to be part of the design of the building. On facing walls in the choir of S. Vitale are the well-known portraits of Justinian and Theodora and their retinues, and although these are portrait groups and have all the richness of a Byzantine court, yet they are so balanced and simple in composition that they too take their place as part of the architectural design. The roughness of texture obtained in the use of tesserae and their placing so that different ones catch the light from different angles as one moves gives a vibrant quality.

Mosaic making

It needs an enormous amount of time to make a ceramic mosaic, for not only does one want many, many tesserae, one usually wants them in many, many colours too and then variations of colours. So I suggest that odd moments over a long period be used to make tesserae so that when ready to start there is a large and mixed supply to hand. Incidentally it is a good idea to vary sizes and also to vary shapes; triangular pieces are immensely useful, so are four-sided pieces with one short side—for example to make a curve.

It is great fun making the pattern, that is the great joy, but setting is more difficult for it needs both care and speed. The method I have found easiest is to have the work prepared (roughly, for it inevitably alters to a certain extent as it is transferred—one changes a colour or a shape), roughen the base, and, using a slow setting cement or plaster, cover a section, one which makes a complete shape, allow it to stiffen slightly, then press in the tesserae. Unless it is a very small mosaic it is better to be cautious and do a bit at a time—clay walls can be used to stop the cement spreading and are easily removed. Remember to alter the angles at which the pieces are set.

Different people use different methods. One will arrange the pieces, press on a sticky sheet and lift the whole design on to a prepared ground; another will work under glass (exasperating, I think!) so the tesserae need not be moved; yet another will fire "walls" to make shapes to be filled in, these forming part of the design.

As with tile pictures it is not necessary to cover the whole surface with ceramic—again grasses can be pressed in, string can be left in, sand can give a different texture.

More fun than either separately is to combine tile and mosaic in one panel, to get the contrast of solid blocks of pattern and tiny sparkling pieces. There are endless possibilities with tremendous scope for experiment, imagination and originality.

Chapter Five

DISHES AND MOULD MAKING

Although this may not sound so exciting as building a pot, and admittedly I find it so, yet it has its own special values. One is that dishes are quickly and easily made and so very useful for making innumerable experiments in decorating—and that can be exciting, sometimes very exciting. Dishes can be useful and beautiful about the house too, so it is worth while learning to make them. But the dish is not entirely one's own if someone else has made the mould—it is someone else's shape, and the form is a very big part of the dish. So mould making must be learnt too, and this is especially worth while, for these can be used in many other ways than to make dishes; for example it is a very great help when a curved base is needed on a piece of coiled modelling, or can be used as a curved section of a slab pot. So mould making first—

Making a mould for a dish

There are two main kinds of moulds for making pressed dishes. There are hollow moulds, so that the clay is pressed inside; and mushroom moulds, where it is pressed on to the outside.

The easiest kind to make is a hollow mould designed to have a flat horizontal rim. The shape is made in solid clay upside down on a board, and must be comparatively shallow and have no sharp angles. As a guide to help in getting a perfectly symmetrical shape it is a good idea to cut it out in cardboard and drawing-pin it to the board—keeping the drawing-pins away from the edge. This means you can feel the edge as you build up the shape, work towards it and cut round it. An asymmetrical shape is less difficult except that its balance, when right way up and standing on its base, must be considered.

The surface of this shape must be absolutely perfect, for on the standard of this depends the ease with which all future dishes are made from it—if there is a fault it will be repeated every time the mould is used. A damp cloth over the top and patted hard helps in the early stages; for final neatening I usually use a scraper.

When quite satisfied put walls round. Material for the walls is a matter of personal preference—some people use lino, some wood, some clay. What is really important is that a reasonable space be left round the clay shape—about an inch is suitable, for it does not make it too heavy but is thick enough to be not easily broken and leaves an area of flat space round the top which is useful when making the dish. Another important point is that the walls must be higher than the highest part of the clay so that the base of the mould will be of reasonable thickness—I would suggest one and a half inches. Personally I use wooden walls, for I have four boards adaptable to most shapes and sizes and keep them especially for mould making, so being constantly in contact with plaster they are never used for anything else. These need coils of clay pressed along the bottom and up the joins at the corners.

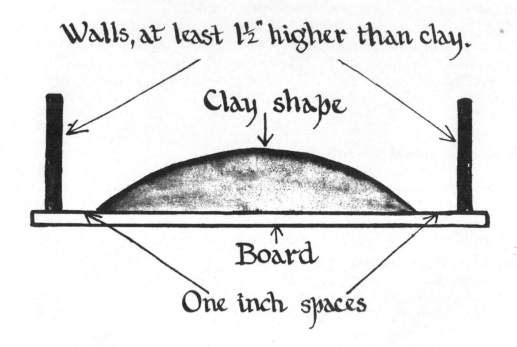

Fig. 35

When ready prepare the plaster, sieving it into the water by rubbing between the hands and mixing it thoroughly so that there are no lumps. When ready pour in. If possible I always have a second person standing by with a lump of plastic clay, just in case of poor wall preparation and a leak. This is disastrous, and messy! Remember to press a finger into the plaster on to the highest point of the clay to measure the thickness. Finally lift the whole board and tap it down gently once or twice to make sure there are no air bubbles left in the plaster, then leave to set.

Calculating the exact amount of plaster to mix is something that can only come with practice. Should there be too little then roughen the surface, make some more as quickly as possible, and add it. So long as the first plaster hasn't finished setting it usually joins well. Plaster can vary between quick or very slow setting—an occasion such as this proves the value of using slow setting plaster. On the other hand, should too much plaster have been made it is an asset rather than a problem for small lumps of plaster are very useful. Either drop it on to the bench in small thick pools, like making drop scones, or pour it into any old small cardboard boxes— those from soap, bath cubes or chocolates. These can be used for making sprigs, for making textures, or pressed patterns for tiles. Never, on any account, pour left-over plaster down the sink!

When the mould is set remove the walls, lift it from the board and turn right way up, and take out the clay, being careful not to damage the surface inside the mould. If the edges need neatening now is the time to do it—it is easier than when it is quite dry. It must, of course, dry out thoroughly before use—a week on top of the kiln is ideal.

Mushroom moulds are the reverse of hollow moulds, that is the shape inside the dish with a foot added. Frequently I make a mushroom mould from the hollow mould, simply by filling the hollow with plaster and, as it begins to set, pressing in a cylinder of thin cardboard and filling this with plaster to about four inches higher. Don't do this last too soon, for if the plaster is still very liquid that in the cylinder will mix with it and overflow. Don't forget to line the hollow mould before starting. Various things can be used to prevent the two moulds from sticking together; I often use a thick layer of slip.

Shapes for mushroom moulds for dishes could also be built up by hand or thrown on the wheel. It is slightly more difficult to make a mould for a dish if the lip is not to be horizontal, for this means it must be made upside down so that it rests on a clay bed with the exact slopes or curves of the rim, and the edges of the clay bed must be cut to take the walls.

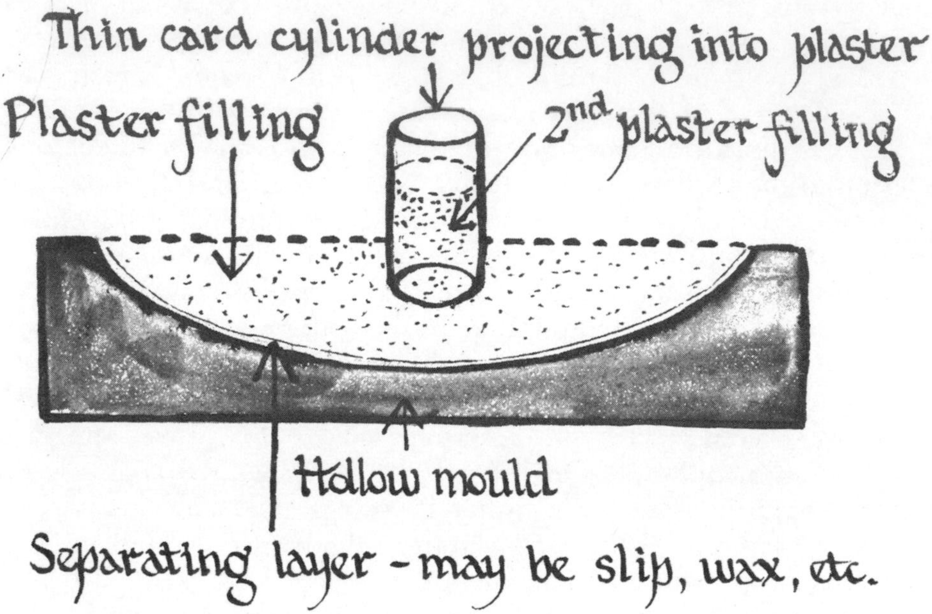

Thin card cylinder projecting into plaster

Plaster filling

2nd plaster filling

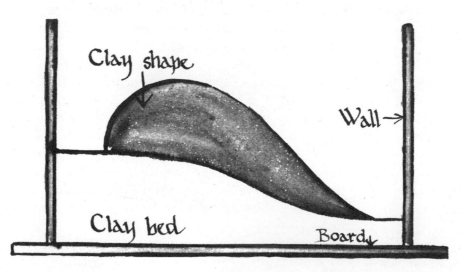

Hollow mould

Separating layer – may be slip, wax, etc.

Fig. 36

Clay shape

Wall →

Clay bed

Board

Making a mould with a rim which is not flat.

Fig. 37

Early moulds

The first moulds were made many hundreds of years ago, not of plaster but of baked clay. Usually these biscuit moulds were fired with the clay pressed in them so that they were constantly being fired. The art of mould making was completely mastered by the potters of Ancient American countries like Peru, Ecuador, Columbia, Mexico, Panama and Costa Rica—the oldest moulded pottery being the Cupisnique. Sometimes the entire piece was moulded. Sometimes only parts were moulded and the rest modelled by hand, as with many Aztec household Gods where only a fairly flat basic shape was pressed and intricate details were modelled and added by hand. Many entire moulds were two-piece; to make the model, the clay was pressed on to the inside of each piece, allowed to dry a little, the two pieces taken out and joined and traces of the join removed as far as possible. Since all these were finished off by hand it is rarely that identical objects have been found although the same mould may have been used over and over again. I have been lucky enough to try one of these moulds;

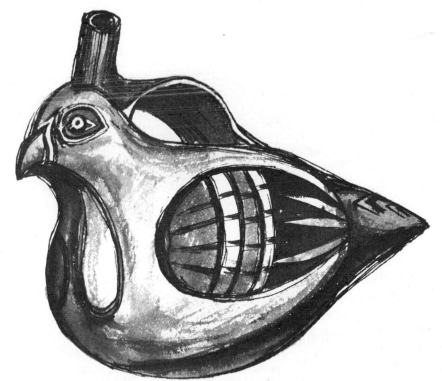

Nazca Water Pot in the shape of a frigate bird.

Fig. 38   By courtesy of the British Museum.

67

perhaps due to inexperience, perhaps because of great respect and care for something over a thousand years old, I found it neither easy nor quick! Many hundreds of water containers in fascinating variety can be seen in the British Museum. Many are painted but many more are modelled in the form of birds and animals—a pair of geese, a dog, a frog, a tortoise, a crocodile. In these bottom and handle were modelled separately and added to the moulded part.

Most of us have found sherds of Roman pottery of various kinds. Much is the beautifully thrown "coarse ware" made in England—superb jars and mortaria, many stamped by the maker; some, red in colour, was imported from Arretium in Italy where pottery was made between approximately 500 B.C. and A.D. 425. Some of this Arretine ware, which became the most common and well-known type of red gloss pottery, was elaborately decorated with patterns in raised relief and was made from 25 B.C. This relief decoration was actually in the mould, which was made of clay and had metal stamps or stamps of biscuited clay pressed into it before it was fired to become a biscuit mould. Most are bowl shaped and had a thrown foot added. The reliefs are just sufficiently high in relation to the curve to come out easily when the clay has shrunk in drying. Many of these designs were influenced by metalwork, for pottery was then regarded as the poor man's equivalent in table ware.

Wooden moulds have already been mentioned in the making of tiles; wood was used both for the tile boxes and the stamping of patterns in medieval times. In fact some tiles, and bricks too, are made in wooden moulds today.

No one is quite sure when plaster of Paris was first used in pottery making. It was first used in England about the middle of the eighteenth century, it is recorded as being used for pottery making in Italy two hundred years earlier, and it had been used before that by Greeks and Romans, but for walls and not for pottery making.

Certainly the discovery of its use with clay made a great difference in the production of pottery, and its value to industry is enormous. As plaster absorbs water quickly shapes are soon ready to be taken out, and as a method of identical repetition where the output is large, it is quick and economical. Very complicated shapes like teapots, coffee jugs and casseroles are all made in this way, sometimes the mould having to be in as many as ten pieces. All deep moulds like these and those for cups, jugs and bowls are intended for making by slip casting. Usually the shapes are designed on paper, made in solid clay, and the moulds made round these. With casting slip the pots can then be reproduced in large numbers and in actual production this is technically very efficient. But it results only too often in rigid, lifeless and mechanical shapes. It need not be so—perhaps wider education can give a knowledge and appreciation of good form and pattern leading to a demand for a better standard.

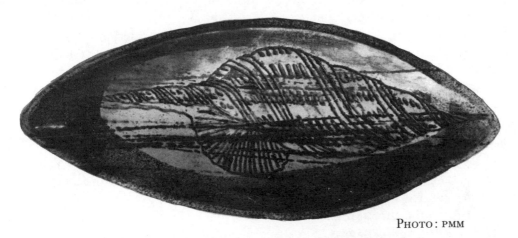

Fig. 39   Simple pressed dish. Shell graffito, then inlay. Masked spraying. Lines made with string. Iron, copper and cobalt used under a matt tin glaze.

Making a dish

For making in a hollow mould a rolling pin, a piece of cloth, a sponge, a wooden modelling tool and a ball of well-wedged clay are needed. The clay is rolled out on the cloth to approximately a quarter of an inch in thickness for a large dish, thinner for a smaller one. Good judgment will come with practice, and with feeling the balance of weight and size in a finished dish —too thin ones are quite as bad and disconcerting as too heavy dishes. Most people have no difficulty in rolling out evenly if reminded that it is not to be treated as pastry and is to be rolled in all directions. This is important, not only in making the clay perfectly even with no ridges, but, more important, in rolling to the shape of the mould. When thin enough and even all over it should be the same shape as the mould but slightly larger to allow for both the curvature and the making of a neat edge. It is a good idea to turn over the clay at least once, probably more often, for not only is it easier but then you will find out if there was a crease in the cloth, if it was over a join in the table, or if there was a crack in the clay. Should things like blisters appear the clay was not properly wedged, for these are air bubbles and must be eliminated—cut them open and press out the air. One other thing—never roll right to the edge of the clay— needing less pressure it will so easily be made thinner, and the edge is the last place which should be weak!

69

When ready lift up the clay on the cloth—or rolling pin, as I find cookery experts do with ease—hold it over the mould and let it down. Peel off the cloth, and with the sponge, starting from the centre and working outwards, gently press it down to the shape of the mould. Smooth it lightly so as to make no impression in the soft clay, and do not go beyond the hollow— leave the edges sticking upwards. If you've miscalculated and there's too much clay, cut it off to about a quarter of an inch above the top of the mould with the wooden tool, keeping it away from the plaster. Then start to neaten the edge. Put the wooden tool flat on to the inch of level plaster left round the top of the mould, hand outside, tool projecting over the hollow of the dish, and, using the fingers of the left hand to lightly hold the clay inside against the edge of the mould, move the tool round the top (see Fig. 40). Be cautious—it is easier to take off a little and do it again, than to take off too much and have to carefully join on more clay. With practice this is easy and extremely quick. The purpose of having the tool projecting right through the clay is to protect the vulnerable inside edges of the mould; the purpose of resting the tool level on the flat top as it is moved round is to ensure that it does not dip down, so making the dish edge, where cracking is most likely, thinner than the rest. Finally run either a damp finger or sponge lightly round the inside of the rim so that it is not sharp but gently rounded. Do not attempt to touch the outside of the rim while the dish is in the mould.

PHOTO: PMM

Fig. 40   Levelling off the edge of a dish.

If the dish is to be decorated with slip this is the time to pour it in. If not, just let it dry until it will slip out easily yet is hard enough to retain its shape. Now is the time to neaten off the outside edge of the rim. If the dish has been well made all it will need is a gentle rub with a damp sponge to take off the sharpness and to round it slightly. It ought to be perfectly level and perfectly even. Should this not be so, then it can be corrected with a sharp metal tool, but be careful not to make an extra plane when doing this. Remember too that as the thin parts cannot now easily be made thicker the thick parts must therefore be made thinner. Sharp edges will occur through shaving these down and must be rounded off with a damp finger or sponge. Check that the dish stands well, for if it wobbles at all it will never be satisfactory in use. So if the base is too curved, first level it with the flat side of a scraper, then, using the round side, make a slight concave hollow in the middle—this will make it stand well.

If the dish is to have feet a rounded base will be more attractive. It is much easier to make dishes which are to have feet over a mushroom mould, for they can be applied at once while the clay is in the same state of plasticity—not as in a hollow mould where it would be necessary to let the dish become stiff enough to maintain its shape when turned out and even to take pressure.

The principle of making over a mushroom mould is very similar—to roll out and press on, but here it helps if the cloth is damp and is used to help smooth the clay over the mould. See there are no creases.

A dish may need feet,
either to make it more stable or improve its
appearance.

Fig. 41

The foot can be a strip or coil added or there can be three or more separate feet. Anything will stand on three feet—four is very much more difficult. These might be simply a ball of clay pressed on and curved into the dish, avoiding trapping air, and pulled to a blunt point. They must not be too sharp or thin or they will be scratchy and will break easily. Or feet might be shaped and modelled, or they could be made in a mould and joined on. Increased stability is given if feet turn outwards. As soon as the clay is hard enough to keep its form and be supported on its feet it will begin to shrink away from the mould and can be lifted off. The inside edge of the rim can now be rounded.

Making dishes really well is quite a quick process, so perfect the technique and get into the rhythm and make several. It is a good idea, for not only is there another to hand in case of a breakage, but also it is surprising how one idea follows another once you start to decorate.

Chapter Six

SLAB BUILDING

A slab pot is built from pieces of clay rolled out and cut to shape. Bernard Leach's definition is that it is "a kind of ceramic joinery, and provided the designs derive from the nature of the material it offers yet another wide range of expression to the studio potter." (*A Potter's Book.*) Being made from cut pieces joined together these become angular pots and can be strong, straight and dignified, yet can so easily give rather hard and insensitive pots in unskilled hands. What makes it one of my favourite methods is that it can so easily and effectively be combined with others. Slab and coil are particularly happy together, for while the straight lines and angles give strength they are softened by the contrast of the rounded curves of the coiling.

Making a slab pot
To a great extent these pots must be preconceived, for it is often necessary to have a pattern. For a simple four-sided rectangular pot this means only two broad and two narrow side pieces and a base.

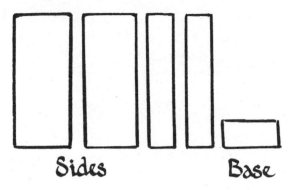

Sides   Base

Fig. 42

Though any clay can be used, as with coiling, an open groggy clay is preferable. The clay is rolled out to about a quarter of an inch in thickness,

73

varying slightly according to the size of the pot. The pieces are cut out with a knife or wooden tool using a ruler or, if necessary, putting on a pattern and cutting round it. When all the pieces are ready—it probably will not have been possible to get them from one piece—they should be put on to a piece of sanded board and left to dry out a little. As soon as they are stiff enough to keep their shape when lifted they are ready to join. Personally I mitre the corners—it gives a larger joining area and is more satisfactory in keeping the shape accurate. When teaching children I let them join the pieces with an end on top of an edge, for they find this easier, and also it eliminates the difficulty of getting an accurate angle in cutting the mitre. Always put the biggest piece and greatest length at the bottom when beginning to join so that it has maximum support. So with the simple rectangular pot one of the wide side pieces would be laid flat, the two narrower ones joined on top of its edges, the base inserted, also on top, at one end (with the non-mitring method for children this would need to be cut shorter). It is absolutely essential that these be placed on top both because if put outside it would not be possible to see all the joins and also the final piece, which can at this stage be added, would be too small to be able to rest on top. It is then safe to stand the pot right way up.

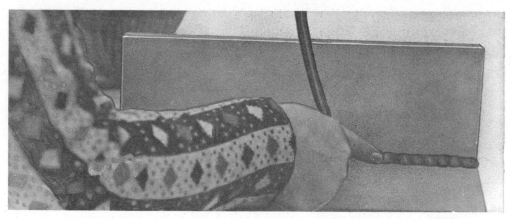

Fig. 43   Joining slabs.

To make the joins, roughen both surfaces where they will touch and about a quarter of an inch on either side, damp them, and repeat this as often as seems necessary with the state of the clay. Once is sufficient if the clay is just right, more often if it has hardened too much. Press the two edges together and smooth the outside firmly with a finger. On the interior angle add a coil. First press it centrally well into the angle so there is no

Fig. 11 "*Mother*" *pot.*

possibility of trapping air, then thumb it down on to both adjacent surfaces. Not only does this strengthen the join but also prevents it from being thinner than the rest of the pot, for doubtless the sharpness of the outside corner will be taken off later. Many people use slip for joining, indeed it is the accepted method, but I have found it far less satisfactory.

Using the method

Many variations can be made using this very simple and obvious basic shape. Made as a box instead of a vase, especially if given four feet so that air can circulate underneath, it could be used as a container for bulbs or potted plants, this being a very suitable shape to fit on a windowsill. Glazing is unnecessary and undesirable for plants, though for bulbs with provision for drainage in the fibre they might be glazed inside, but normally the red clay is pleasing and attractive with the green of foliage. Keeping the red clay colour only, incised patterns simply and clearly cut are ideal decoration and so are patterns in low relief. Lug handles, perhaps modelled, might be suggested for lifting. Large "boxes" for plants look wonderful outside, on terraces, in porches, near French windows or perhaps on a low wall.

Illustration 44 is one of the "mother" pots made by an eleven-year-old form. Each child rolled out and cut a slab approximately twelve by four and a half inches and a quarter of an inch thick. Built on this in low relief and textured was an illustration of Mother working—there was a choice of mother or father but twenty-two out of twenty-three were "mothers"! Groups of four joined their slabs together, added a base and then a foot at each corner. They are glazed inside.

Enormous differences are made by the addition of feet or spouts, for example, when a tall rectangular vase is finally joined and standing coils can be added to the top—perhaps to curve inwards and then upwards as in the bottle illustrated as No. 45 by a fifteen-year-old girl. When adding coils in this way always check that the pot is still soft enough to take the first one—if any doubt, roughen and dampen the top edge and about $\frac{3}{4}$-in. down as for joining sides.

The rectangular shape could be made complete by adding the sixth side across the top and, if a vase, a decorative pattern of holes could be cut into the flat top so that tall flowers with long thin stems could be arranged more easily.

Variations of shape

Naturally any number of sides can be used; four is the most obvious and the simplest. I started the hard way and my first slab pot had eight sides almost twenty inches tall and only two and a half inches wide, with coiling

Fig. 45   Ann's slab pot.

added—I wished I hadn't—but made it in the end! Some people make very complicated jugs and teapots involving positively scores of slabs, but unless these are extremely well designed they are apt to look messy and over-complicated. Three is a particularly attractive number and especially so for bottle shapes with long thin triangular sides.

Five is a very good number too, though more difficult to handle. An example is illustrated here. If the five sides are of different widths they give unending variety and great pleasure in handling. Nor need they all be of the same height, but in this case the form will almost certainly have to be created as it grows, and adjustments with coils or ledges will have to be made and can only be for the individual pot.

Fig. 46 Students five sided pot.

78

Another thing which children love to do is to experiment with an asymmetric shape joined to another by a strip two or three inches wide. The easiest way is to design a pleasing shape, cut it out twice, put one piece down flat, join a three-inch-wide strip vertically, and join the other side on the top—if a wide shape, it may be necessary to support the top pieces inside with newspaper until it can be stood upright. In order to avoid the necessity for this it is a good idea to make the two big pieces first and allow them to dry a little before making the strip, for this must be slightly softer in order to curve round the shape without cracking. Leave an opening at the top to put the coil in the interior angle of the final piece and also to make the lip, perhaps using coils, perhaps adding a thrown neck and lip or a thrown base also.

Christine's flat shapes.

Fig. 47

Also when upright—and well joined—it will make the pot much more attractive in appearance if a hand is again inserted and the sides tapped gently until they bulge outwards and are slightly rounded.

Slab pottery can be even simpler than any of the preceding suggestions. The tall pots in Fig. 48 are first efforts by eleven-year-olds. They are just a ball of clay rolled out, curved round the rolling pin, cut where the edges meet and pinched together. The decoration was done by pressing in stones while the rolling pin was still inside for support. The remaining clay was rolled flat for a base, the cylinder slipped off and pinched on to it. The inside is glazed matt black.

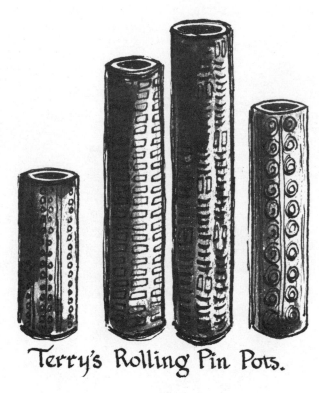

Terry's Rolling Pin Pots.

Fig. 48

Curved slabs

Pieces for slab pots need not be flat. After rolling they can be shaped, perhaps by hand and supported; perhaps on a mound of sand; perhaps, if a definite angle is wanted, over a strip of wood, in this case taking care that the angle is not so acute that the clay will split. The easiest and probably the best way to shape them is by using a mould, and this is one of the many ways, other than making dishes, in which both hollow and mushroom moulds can be very useful.

Fig. 49   Slab and thrown pots: Linda, Janet and Mandy.

These bottles were made by children as an exercise using slabs plus a thrown shape, given after being asked for what seemed the hundredth time by a puzzled child struggling to master the wheel, "Miss Winterburn, what is this grey thing in the bottom of my pot?" Of course—the wheelhead—the thumb pressed too far down yet again. We must use these things; we had enough plant pots; bottles came next. So using a dish mould two identical shapes were made and the edges joined, a piece cut off one end for standing (for which a base piece was rolled and added), and a piece cut off the other end and softened ready to attach the thrown spout. After all the making of an elegant spout was good throwing practice, many adaptations soon appeared, and slab bottles of infinite variety have been popular ever since.

These slab bottles with two curved sides are perfectly simple and very easy to make, for the edges to be joined, as when flat slabs are used, are also flat and level and rest on one another. With three or more sides it is much more difficult, for it is no longer possible to use moulds with a flat horizontal top since they will not fit together, though if the clay is still soft enough to bend it is possible; or if coils or small triangular slabs can be fitted into the spaces it can also be done. So normally these will be built up entirely by hand and individually. Invention and adaptability are invaluable—but take away the evidence of the supports used; a missing bowl of water was once found inside a completed narrow-spouted bottle— mine! Personally if I have wanted to repeat a shape often enough to warrant a special mould, and this happens rarely, I have built the shape by hand and cast from it. No doubt it is also mathematically possible to work out the angles from a design and mould a side. I confess to never having done this, though sketches and drawings of all kinds are at all times of immense value in stimulating ideas for form, as for pattern. I like to see the thing I am making in the round and to be able to adapt it as it grows.

Slab building is also a wonderful method for ceramic sculptures; also, perhaps especially, if combined with coiling; both using flat cut pieces and pieces from moulds—whole or part moulds, which, of course, need not necessarily be joined rim to rim. BEWARE—this has infinite possibilities in use but even more for misuse, and many badly designed, complicated and incoherent "constructions" are the result!

Chinese stoneware bottles
Slab building is a method which has been primarily associated with the Far East, and in many museums there are examples which are well worth study. In the Victoria and Albert Museum there are T'ang bottles made about the eighth century from two-piece biscuit moulds. They are strong and broad at the base, with a foot added so that they stand well, and taper upwards towards the narrow spouts. Decoration consists of incised patterns, simple like the shapes, covered by a cream-coloured glaze. There is a Sung bottle in the same museum evidently made in a biscuited mould which was incised so that the clay pressed into it has a pattern in relief.

There are several contemporary studio potters who are working primarily in slab pottery.

Fig. 50   Three-sided slab bottles: Mollie Winterburn.

Chapter Seven

THROWING AND TURNING

This is a method better seen than described in words or even with pictures. Furthermore it is somewhat outside the scope of school pottery. some schools having no wheel and others very few, certainly never enough to make it an activity for a normal sized class. Personally I keep it as a privilege for older girls, after a course of handbuilt work, if they wish it, or for girls taking examinations which insist on mastery of the wheel, or, very rarely, for a girl with exceptional ability or whose work seems to lend itself to thrown shapes. These all work very hard in their spare time, for practice is essential, and some do become expert.

PHOTO: PMM

Fig. 51   Shapes from practice on the wheel: Elaine.

The wheel has a strange attraction, the same fascination as watching the wake of a ship, the breaking of waves on the shore, the movement of wind across a field of wheat. Perhaps it is the continuous movement and change of shape—many people are satisfied just to watch and many seem bewitched by the soft movement of clay between their hands. Besides, it always looks so easy!

The first essential is well-wedged clay. The second to centre it, and it is soon found that the one place to which the clay has an intense objection is

Fig. 52   Ann's pot made from two separately thrown pieces with a pulled handle.

the exact centre. This is where practice is needed—once centred it is so easy to make a pot and until then utterly useless to begin to shape it. It must be watched and tried; as with coiling people will find their own method. Points to remember when thinning the walls are to leave a reasonable thickness for the foot, to make the base the right size immediately, to make the lifting movement even and steady and always from the very bottom to the very top, to keep the top slightly smaller than the bottom, and, though there should not be a noticeable difference, to have the walls just very, very slightly thicker towards the base to evenly support the weight of clay. When shaping remember also to keep the movement always even and right from bottom to top, and, if collaring, not to do it too suddenly or it will ripple. When making a bowl remember to start with a wide shallow curve, and that generally a bowl must be thrown quite quickly or there is a tendency to flare outwards.

The lip is extremely important and an ill-considered unsuitable one can ruin an otherwise good shape. Take care about this—will it help if the lip turns in and downwards into the shape or will it be better to shape it upwards into a convex curve to carry on the shape of the pot over the top? On the other hand should it be emphasised as a definite stop in the growth of the form by a sudden outward thrust? Can a ridge lend emphasis, should details of a profile draw attention to the top, should it become squarer or thinner, or should it be turned right over to give strength? All these can give character to a pot.

Turning

Most potters finish off the base of their pots when they are leather-hard by turning them upside down on the wheel, pressing down a coil of clay to keep them steady, shaping with a sharp tool and, if they want one, making a foot. Remember to check the thickness of the base before starting. If the pot is very small at the lip, as a bottle, use a chuck, which is a cylinder of raw clay, to support it. As throwing, this is a process which must be seen, not described. Most people turn off as little as possible just to make it neat and leave no sharp edges, believing that the throwing should be perfect and complete and that it is bad pottery if it needs a lot of turning; others count on a certain amount of turning as an essential part of their method of working. Many Greek pots, which are so thin and so carefully and precisely shaped, are turned a great deal. Turning tools should be kept sharp—many people use one favourite but some like to have a pointed, a square, and a rounded turning tool. As with lips a great variety in shape of foot is possible, they may be thick or thin, deep or shallow, they may go straight down for strength, out for stability, or even in to continue the line of the pot.

These are only a few hints—no attempt has been made to describe throwing and turning—they simply must be seen and practised. I would just like to emphasise the importance of practice to get complete control. A beginner tends to be satisfied with any shape and is just happy to have a "pot"! This is fatal, for until there is complete mastery of the machine exploration of form cannot begin, but once it is there then assurance and speed in handling will give vigour and vitality to the growth of the pot.

Photo: pmm

Fig. 53   Jennifer's coffee set.

It is essential too to consider function, where it will be best to join the handle, how deeply to inset the lid and how much it must go inside the pot to prevent it falling off in pouring, whether there will be an even flow to the lip of a jug and whether it will pour without dribbling, whether the base is broad enough in relation to the rest to be stable, whether a spout will be tall enough not to overflow when a coffee pot is full, to remember, for good cooking, it might be sensible to leave the base of a casserole thick, not to have the lid too high or the handle jutting out too much for the oven. All these things must be considered, and only added to beauty of form will they make a really good pot.

Chapter Eight

HANDLES, SPOUTS AND LIDS

Handles

Pottery making has evolved for and from use, so, from practical necessity in the course of time, the shape of a pot became more and more suited to its purpose. To make it easier to carry or even to sling over the shoulder adaptations were made, and so we get lugs and handles.

European prehistoric

Central European Neolithic pottery shows this development very well. The earliest "spiral culture" ones have simply a projection to make lifting easier, some have projections with hollows into which a stick may be fitted, some have attractive zoomorphic lugs round which string for lifting could be tied, and some are perforated so that string can go through. Then there are handles—squat broad handles, tall thin ones called ribbon handles, and curiously shaped ones which look winged.

Projections for lifting

Fig. 54

Ancient American

Handles and spouts are often combined in pots from Ancient America and were, like the handles in Fig. 55, obviously made for ease in carrying.

No one is quite certain how these were made, though some people feel they were probably modelled over something soft and pliable like grass which would burn out in the firing. Often these handles were set into the pot so that they actually project a little way inside. This makes a much better join than simply being added to the pot's surface.

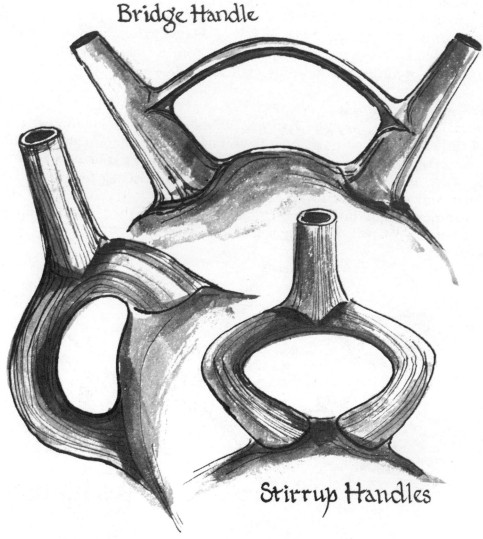

Fig.55   By courtesy of the British Museum.

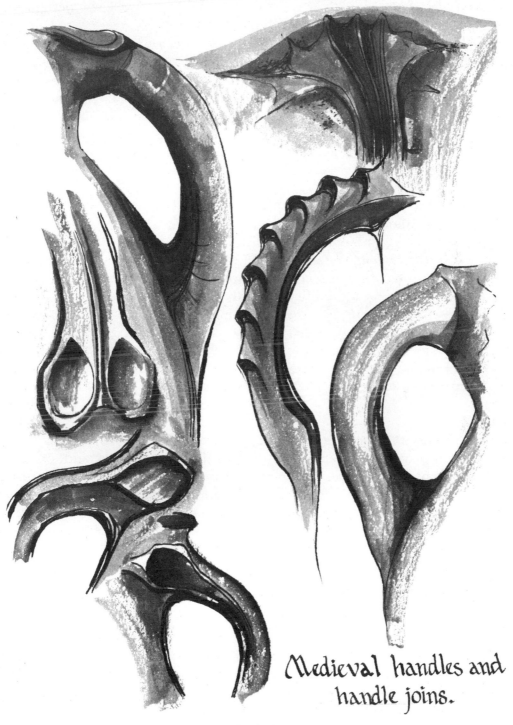

Medieval handles and
handle joins.

Fig. 56

89

Medieval English

In English Medieval pottery also, handles are very much a part of the pot and superbly well joined. They look solid and firm and easy to grasp—good qualities in use. When attached they were pressed from the inside as well as the outside and the ends firmly splayed out. Several have been found which have an arrangement of holes so that some of the clay of the handle actually does go through the wall of the pot. In shape they are frequently quite round, and sometimes they are almost rectangular like a leather strap. The top ridge is often pinched up into scallops, not merely for decoration but, like the general tendency of pottery of the period, for a very practical reason, i.e. to lessen the risk of splitting.

Maltese prehistoric

Some of the best and loveliest Prehistoric pots I have ever seen are in Valletta in the National Museum of Malta. Amongst these are some which have a type of handle not seen elsewhere—a tunnel handle. These are exceptionally strong, being really part of the pot for they are modelled inside the wall. Usually there are two, sometimes more. This has a further advantage in that it does not interrupt the profile of these fine pots. Similar tunnels are found cut in rock at ground level, and also in the walls and doorways of temples, and the former could have been used, perhaps, for tethering, and the latter for hanging a curtain.

Greek

Greek pottery too shows an enormous variety not only in the shape but also in the placing of lugs and handles, as, for example, the sudden sharp strong accent of an absolutely horizontal pair of handles on a Corinthian cup. Indeed most cups had horizontal handles, this making them easier to lift when lying on a couch. In fact all Greek handles were very practical and were designed for convenience in use. They were big and strong, sometimes very big, and in their curves and the way they were joined, and also in their decoration, were made to be part of the whole form of the pot.

Only a few of the enormous variety of different types of handles which can be seen in many museums have been mentioned. Handles in themselves can form a fascinating subject of study and making a handbuilt pot gives a wonderful opportunity to experiment.

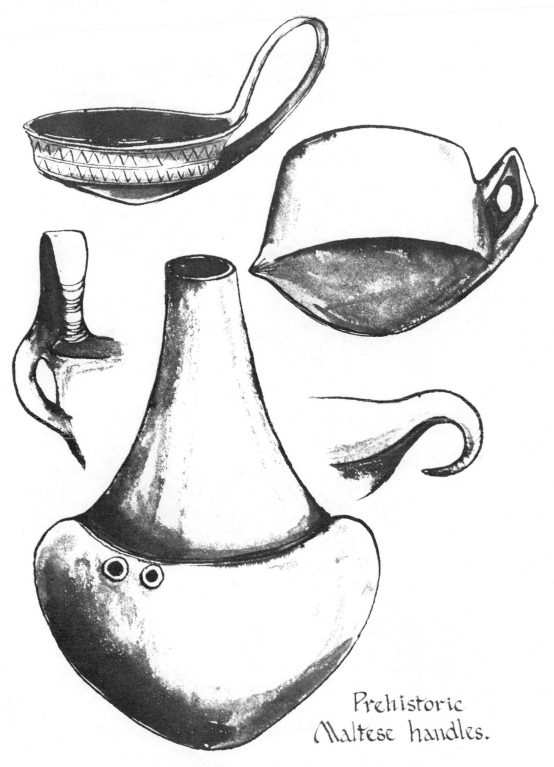

Prehistoric
Maltese handles.

Fig. 57   By courtesy of the National Museum of Malta.

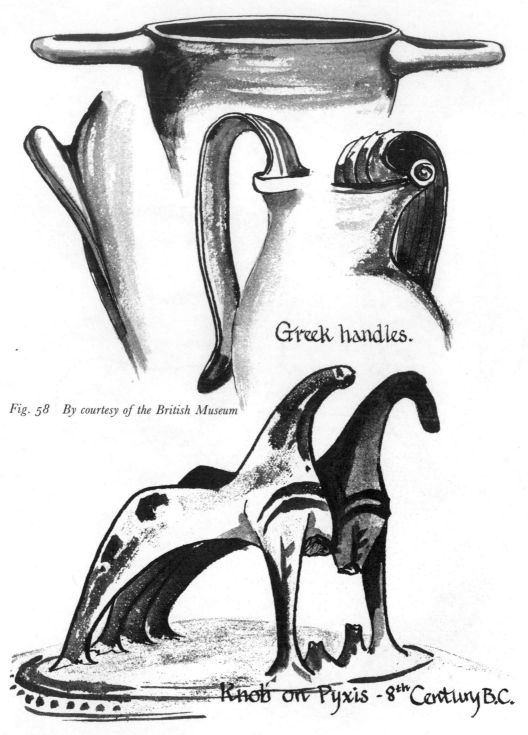

Greek handles.

Fig. 58   By courtesy of the British Museum

Knob on Pyxis - 8th Century B.C.

Fig. 59

Making a pulled handle

Normally a pulled handle would look out of place on a handbuilt pot but would be the only right one for a thrown pot—though, of course, there are exceptions to every rule. Pulled handles are certainly the most suitable on cups, mugs and jugs for everyday use and are quick and easy to make.

Take some fairly stiff clay, tap it into a wedge shape, hold the thick end in one hand, wet the other hand and with it grasp the thinner edge and smoothly and firmly pull it downwards. Continue this movement, turning the hand which is holding the clay as necessary to keep the shape even. Always be conscious of the final shape; if a perfectly round section is wanted then the pulling until it is of the right thickness is simple and even, but if any other shape is wanted, such as an oval or strap shape which are slimmer and more graceful, or with one or two ridges, then it is well to be conscious of this from the first pull. Make the ridges firmly with pressures from the thumb as it moves down the length of clay.

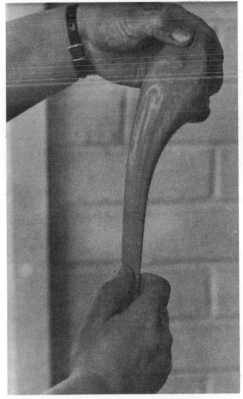

PHOTO: PMM

Fig. 60 Pulling a handle.

PHOTO: PMM

Fig. 61   Beryl's jug and jar.

Some people attach the wedge and pull the handle on the pot, others pull the handle first and then attach it. In either case it is the thicker top end which is joined to the pot first, and even if the shape has already been completed a final pull from the top before attaching the lower end helps to keep the curve strong and vigorous—for there is nothing worse than a sagging curve for giving an impression of weakness. Timidity and indecision show, so press it down firmly and clearly at the lower end. Incidentally the pot should be still fairly damp when the handle is joined, for if not then the handle will contract much more in drying and will split—if there is any doubt join the handle at the top and let it contract a little before making the second join. The most important thing of all is to join the handle at a suitable place. Perhaps in throwing a ridge will have been left near to the top of the pot so that the handle can be joined into this with its end splayed and the line round the pot continued into and down the handle

Placing and size are of supreme importance and can only be considered separately for each pot. A handle too small for the fingers is useless, one too large will not balance well. Character can be given to the pot by the way in which it fits—whether it blends into the curve or makes an aggressive thrust into space. It cannot be emphasised too much that handles, like spouts and knobs, are very much a part of the shape of the whole pot.

94

Lugs

For a heavy pickling jar lug handles will be best, for the weight is held nearer the pot. They are also better on casseroles where oven space has to be considered. A very simple, quick and easy way to make them is to roll a short thick coil, taper it at both ends, pat it flat, cut one edge straight, bend it into a semi-circle, and attach the straight edge. As with ordinary handles see that the edge thickens where it joins so that it curves into the pot and the line of the semi-circle can continue into the pot.

Spouts

These can be modelled, moulded, cast or thrown. If a spout is to be straight it can be thrown, if it is to have definite curves it is better to make a mould and cast from this. Always remember that the aim is that it should pour well, so the pouring edge will have to be fairly sharp and it should taper. If it is for a teapot, instead of one hole where it is joined, perforations are better for they help to hold back the tea leaves.

Lids

Lids too must be related to the shape of the pot and can either continue the line of growth without an obvious break, forming a cover, make an angle with the pot, sitting on top, or be inset. If not inset they must have some kind of flange to prevent them from slipping off. If the pot is thrown and is to have an inset lid, leave a socket or ledge on to which the lid can fit and make the lid immediately afterwards, so that they will dry evenly together. Some people have amazingly accurate eyes but it is surprising how wrong one can be, and generally better to use callipers to ensure a snug fit. Another point to remember is to be generous with the flange— especially for something like a teapot which will be tilted in use. Lids can be thrown right way up and completed at once—this is a suitable method for one which is to be pulled into a kind of spout with an airhole, as for a casserole; but generally lids are thrown upside down with a good thickness of clay left underneath which can later be turned into the knob. If insufficient clay is left a ball can be added and turned or modelled, or modelling can be added.

Chapter Nine

COMBINING METHODS

A brief note

The preceding chapters—pinch, coil, slab, dish and tile making and throwing, are basic, simple handbuilt methods. Once known and mastered they can be adapted to personal needs and used according to individual requirements. Especially methods of making can be combined so that no hand building, providing its form is suitable for the nature of the material, is out of reach.

These are only the tools necessary to begin work. Sensitivity to form and pattern and a clear mind are essential for inspiration; enthusiasm and hard work are very necessary. As one constantly will meet criticism and, possibly, opposition one must also have absolute conviction. Unless ideas are carried out they are lost; if outside ideas are allowed to interfere the work will become weak, insincere and unconvincing. Be of independent thought and work to fulfil your intention—with the obvious condition that if the result is not satisfactory it will be destroyed. Just as one goes through sketches and drawings every year or so and destroys those which are of no use, or have not followed the line of development, so with pottery.

Use whatever is necessary to carry out ideas. Some methods combine more happily than others—like tile and mosaic, pinch and coil, or slab and coil—but all can be used and adapted as desirable. If the result does not suit the medium it will be obvious at once—and every really good potter has a hammer. Without experiment there can be no achievement.

Work in pottery and ceramic sculpture may be preconceived, but most likely only partly so and the idea will develop as it grows. This is real creative building and real enjoyment.

Fig. 62   Ann's slab, coil and thrown pot.

Chapter Ten

DECORATION

Even in the earliest known pottery the potter was soon not satisfied merely to make a shape of practical use, it had to be as beautiful as possible too. So it was marked with his finger nail, punctured with a stick, or impressed with a stone or shell. Later spirals were incised, then triangles and zigzags and other geometric patterns; and painting using differently coloured earths soon followed.

Nowadays people are much more hesitant about decoration! So often a shape is conceived but with no real idea of its final appearance. True, it may be a superb form, complete in itself and having no need of decoration, but only too frequently it is left undecorated not from choice but from sheer lack of ability to decide what to do or how to do it. The simply bewildering number of possibilities is in itself an obstacle.

Methods using the clay itself

Some decoration can be added at almost all stages in the making of a pot, but if the surface is to be cut or textured in any way or if more clay is to be applied, then it must be done while the clay is still soft and plastic.

Textures The clay can be rolled or pressed on to a surface which will give it a texture. Some lovely marks we have found and used have been made with wood, especially the bark; by grasses laid on a board; by a corn cob rolled round; and by a piece of rock full of fossils. These are natural textures, but man-made ones are usable too—clay rolled over a cane or rush chair seat, cloth of various kinds; string laid on the bench and shredded string; coins pressed in; clay pressed on, a pattern cut and scratched into a block of plaster, or from a road surface. The lovely asymmetric marks made by stones have been mentioned in making tile pictures, by using different facets—ten or twenty different ones from one stone. All kinds of shells are useful, sea shells and shells from nuts, and many kinds of seeds and seed cases which can easily be found wild or in the garden. Brazil nuts, walnuts and date stones are always useful.

Fig. 63   Asymmetric "Brazil nut" pot: Mollie Winterburn.   99

Adding Clay Coils and dots like those on the big Cretan storage jars are simple, bold and effective decoration admirably suited to those impressive large jars. Care must be taken to see that these are really well joined, so the clay of the body should preferably be still soft. Usually a stick or stone has been used to press it on, serving the double purpose of adding a pattern and making a firmer joining.

Saxon Cinerary Urn.

Fig. 64

Nearly all Anglo–Saxon pottery was hand made and rather low fired. Most examples found are from burials and are of two types; small accessary vessels found near a skeleton and placed there for ceremonial reasons which are quite plain; and large urns used for ashes after cremation. It is the latter which are frequently of superb form and vigorous decoration. They have been found mainly in East Anglia and date from the time of the earliest settlers. The shapes grow in a deep wide curve, then turn in from the shoulder to the neck, and it is this upper area which is so richly decorated and which has the lively contrast of relief and impressed pattern. Generally the relief mouldings were formed from the inside by pressing out the clay into knobs and curved ribs, sometimes giving the effect of bosses and arches. Sometimes ribs were applied outside and given a corded pattern. Grooves were produced with a pointed tool of wood or bone and the spaces between these incised lines filled with impressed stamps. Their use seems to be entirely decorative, though some stamps certainly include what must have originally been sun symbols and the fylfot is frequently recognisable.

Slabs can also be added to the surface of the pot in the same way as coils, though greater care is needed to avoid trapping air underneath, as is also the case when adding sprigs.

Making sprigs is one of the uses for the lumps of plaster left over when too much is made for a mould. A shape is carved into the plaster, clay pressed in (don't use the first one—it will be plastery), levelled off across the top, taken out (the mould being of plaster which is absorbent and the shape being shallow it dries sufficiently to remove immediately), and put on to the prepared damped and roughened part of the pot.

Janet's sprigged cruet

Fig. 65

Another less traditional sprig is made by cutting a shape from the plaster, scratching a pattern into it, pressing it into a thinly rolled slab of clay and cutting out the shape. An attraction is that this sprig can be used above the surface in the usual way and also pressed into the surface, thus giving greater variety and contrast in levels and so adding more interest in the use of light and shade.

Another useful way of getting rid of excess plaster is to pour it into the cardboard cylinders in which rolled papers are posted. Tear off the cardboard as soon as the plaster has set, as it is difficult to get off once it dries. Cut the plaster into short lengths, and there are several cylinders ready to be used for rolled decoration. Try making just one cut first and see how it looks, then another and roll it again, gradually building up the pattern.

Shirley's jug.

Fig. 66

Interest was added to this child's quite small coiled jug (Fig. 66) by using her dog as a model for the handle. Children are usually thrilled to have the opportunity to combine modelling with their pottery, and handles and knobs are ideal. Seeing an illustration of horses on the lid of an Athenian covered pot of *c.* 800 B.C. (Fig. 59) may be an immediate inspiration for some form of lidded pot to provide a base for their own modelling. In all historical periods this delight in showing living things is evident—in the animal lugs on a prehistoric jar; the dragon handles on a T'ang vessel; and in the enormous variety of modelling on medieval jugs, the man pulling his beard, the man playing a pipe, or the aquamanile (a horizontal ewer) of the knight on horseback, all so typical of the period in their lively observation and vigour of execution.

Fig. 67 shows decoration in low relief in a combined effort by three children. Each child in the form rolled out a slab a good $\frac{1}{4}$-in. thick and, using the spare clay cut off in getting the piece to the desired shape and size, built up their reliefs from a previously made sketch, and combined

Fig. 67   Three-sided slab pot with low relief decoration: combined work of three children.

together in groups of three or four to join their sides and add a base and feet or top to suit their shape.

Subtracting Clay Just as clay can be added so it can be taken away. The simplest form of this is an incised line. Bronze Age pottery from Cyprus is often decorated in this way, the thickness of the line unvaried but bands having different spacing and using zigzags, chevrons and dots. Cut through the polished surface it also gives a contrast in surface texture.

The incised line was used with exquisite control in China during the Sung Period, the lines being free and flowing and varied in width and depth, and always very fine, delicate and sensitive. Flowers and birds were most frequently used as a basis for pattern.

Carole's pattern for a carved bowl.

Fig. 68

The variation of width and depth in cutting can be extended until it is no longer an incised line but a carved surface. Numerous examples of this are found in the pottery of Ancient Central America. The Tepeu phase of the Maya was one of great variety in pottery making, as it was also a great period in astronomy and architecture. There were tall cylindrical pots, bowls, flaring dishes, and many pots with tripod feet. The polychrome vessels are very spectacular, but also typical of the period is monochrome pottery where perhaps a band, but sometimes the whole pot, was covered with carved low relief. Sometimes there were scenes from Maya ceremonial life; often the pattern was based on hieroglyphs, though these are not usually inscriptions but have just been used decoratively and are meaningless. For carving it is better to let the clay become leather-hard and to use a metal tool.

Making holes This carving can be carried further to cut through the clay so that holes form part of the decoration. Of course this can only be done when it does not in any way detract from the use of the pot. The flower holder in Fig. 69 is intended as a table decoration, and the holes, in addition to being carefully designed from a decorative point of view, are also for use and are planned for flower arrangement, and none is placed so low as to prevent a reasonable amount of water being contained in the pot. Holes are also both useful and decorative in making lamps to give a subdued light, for which handbuilt pottery is particularly suitable.

Many pots can be found in which the potter has made holes and taken care that they are well filled with glaze so that light shows through although they are completely waterproof. Chinese bowls where rice has been pressed into the thin clay are examples of this; the rice burns out but its place is

PHOTO: FRS

Fig. 69   Jennifer's flower-holder.

taken by the glaze. Islamic potters between the ninth and twelfth centuries were absolute masters in using light, and made wonderful pots where complicated bands of plant patterns were cut right through the sides and filled in by a thick transparent glaze, so giving the effect of a traceried window.

Using colours

Pottery colours are obtained from metal oxides. Infinite variety can be achieved by the use of only two or three oxides, not just by mixing but because the colour is also affected by the firing and to an enormous extent by the glaze. Normally in teaching I use only four for painting, though others are available if a child wishes to experiment with them. They are:

Iron oxide: with tin glazes gives warm browns to dark reddish browns, and with a clear lead-based glaze it will give a yellowish brown.

Manganese dioxide gives black on red clay, purplish brown on buff or white.

Cobalt oxide always gives blues. It is very expensive but very strong, so that only small quantities are used.

Copper oxide gives greens, but reds in a reduced firing. Since it is a black powder you may well be met with disbelieving looks when children using it for the first time are told it is green, especially as when it comes out of the biscuit firing it looks brown!

Any of these can be mixed and all have certain peculiarities which will be found in use. Here are a few things to remember:

Cobalt is so strong and intense it should rarely be used alone; softened by iron it makes an attractive greenish blue, and with manganese a soft dark purplish grey blue. Iron under a lead glaze tends to dissolve and disappear so must be used thickly, but if too thick under a tin glaze will break up. Iron with copper makes the green less bluish. Manganese will make black if mixed with a little cobalt or iron or copper—I use Manganese 5: Iron 1: Cobalt 1. Chrome oxide will give from dark to lovely grey greens but with lead glazes can give bright yellow and with lead and lime an absolutely horrible pink! Nickel oxide makes a pleasant grey green, and iron chromate an attractive yellowish grey under tin glaze. Tin oxide is very useful for making white opaque glazes and so is titanium. Antimoniate of lead gives excellent yellows but unfortunately cannot be used in schools as it is poisonous. Yellow underglaze I have not found to be an

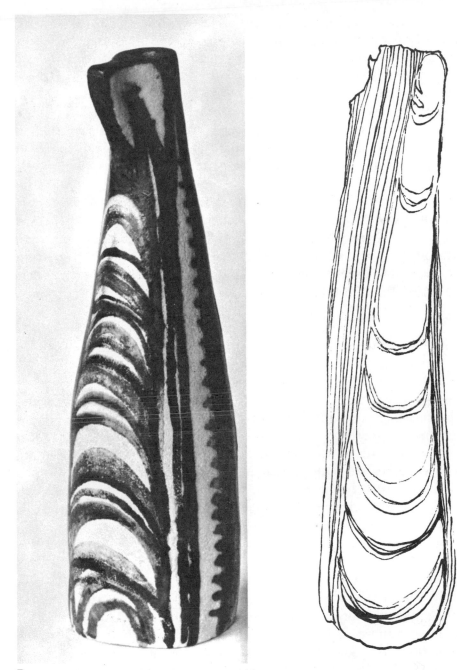

Fig. 70   Marion's pot based on a drawing of a razor shell. Painted.

attractive substitute used on its own but mixed with other oxides in small quantities it can be pleasant.

Some people have large quantities of metal oxides ready mixed with water for fluid brushwork; but, perhaps from personal method of application, I have always found it simpler to have the oxides dry in a palette and have water available so that as the brush goes from water to palette both the thickness and the mixing can easily be varied. While in mass production this would be most unsuitable, it is very good for individual pieces. A point to remember when teaching is to advise taking a little—if insufficient it is easy to get more, if too much it is difficult to put back—it may be damp, also since so many oxides appear black it is easy to muddle them.

Brushwork on pottery can be seen in most museums and collections. It is an enormously wide subject covering work from almost every period and every country. Particularly to be noted are Chinese, Persian and Hispano–Moresque. Each makes a delightful subject for study and each has its own particular excellencies—the flow of the Chinese, the liveliness of the Islamic and the extraordinary strength and vigour of the Hispano–Moresque.

Most people associate only a brush with the application of colour in spite of the immense skill needed to use one really well. Yet it can be applied with almost anything—potato cuts are just as effective on pottery as on cloth or paper, a matchstick can be used end or sideways on. The use of a sponge and spray are obvious and are easily combined with shapes cut in paper and damped to keep them down. A piece of string dipped in the wet oxide can be laid on the clay or dragged across it; and an old dish-cloth used to wipe up the colour can be draped round the pot. Colour can be thrown on—then it will certainly follow the form of the pot. When there is a texture a fairly dry brush dragged across will emphasize it; where a pattern has been incised colour can be brushed into it and scraped off so giving another completely different quality of line (inlay).

Using slip
Slip is liquid clay. If it is slip which is to be used for decorating (about 55% water), unlike slip for casting, it must "fit" the pot. This means not only that it must adhere to the clay of the body but that it must shrink the same amount at the same rate, so it is a good thing to use a powdered form of the body clay for a base. Discarded dried out unfired pottery can be broken up into pieces and used for making slip. Sometimes our slip is made very simply from 60% ball clay and 40% china clay (both powdered), but rather less china clay with the addition of a little Cornish stone and flint is better. They are sprinkled into water (about 2 parts water to 1 part powdered clay), stirred, sieved through a 60 sieve into another container,

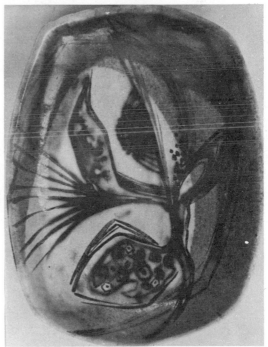

Photos: pmm

Fig. 71   Different inspirations for dish designs—Scythian buckle, railway lines and bursting seedpod.

then through a 100 sieve back into the first container. Newly made slip should not be used straight away—it is better if left for a month and then resieved as before when needed for use. If the slip is for coating then it should just coat a finger if dipped in; if for trailing it needs to be thicker and should drop stiffly from a spoon.

When making coloured slips the percentage of oxides added must be calculated from the dry weight of the other ingredients and should be ground before use. Too many colours are a source of danger—as in painting—though there are exceptions to every rule and on some of the Ancient South American pots as many as fifteen differently coloured slips may be found. Normally three will be found to be the ideal number—red, black and white are always attractive.

Red can be made from red powdered body or by adding 10% iron oxide to the white powdered body.

Black by either 7% manganese and 1% cobalt to the red, or 6% manganese, 1% cobalt, 1% copper, 1% iron to the white.

The following colours are percentages for use with a white powdered body:

Blue 0.5% to 2% cobalt.

Green 4% chrome plus 4% nickel.

Brown 7% manganese plus 2% iron.

Grey 8% iron chromate *or* 3% manganese 3% iron 1% cobalt to be used under a tin glaze.

All slip must be added to the clay when it is barely leather-hard. If the pot or dish is too hard it will split. This is a great danger if the pot is actually dipped, but even if the trailing or painting with slip is done direct on to the body this should be still damp.

Slips have a tendency to dissolve into the glaze during firing so should not be used too thinly unless that particular effect is wanted.

Slip has very often been used simply as a base on which to paint. Where potters found the colour of their body clay unattractive the outside would be covered with slip by dipping. Practice is needed to immerse the pot quickly and accurately, for it is dangerous to have to dip a second time, e.g. if it was not quite horizontal—the slip might be too thick and flake off or the second immersion may mean that the pot absorbs too much moisture so goes soft and loses shape. Perhaps two-thirds of a pot may be dipped; or perhaps the pot might be turned on its side and just dipped into the surface so that there is a round or oval patch of slip—this is called window slipping.

If a dish is to be lined with slip and the dish is made in a hollow mould, the slip can be poured in, the mould tilted if necessary to cover the entire surface, and poured out again—also quite quickly and also while the clay is still damp. If the mould to be used is a mushroom mould then obviously it is better to do the slip decoration immediately the clay is rolled out, let it dry a little and then invert the clay over the mould.

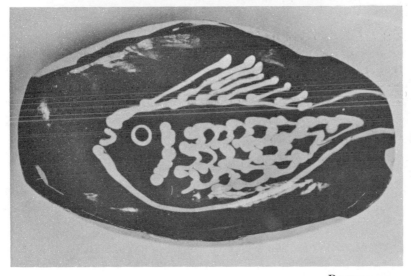

PHOTOS: PMM

Fig. 72   Two dishes decorated with slip; Elizabeth's (top) carved into grey slip, Ann's slip trailed.

If cutting and incising through slip to the body clay, the pot should be allowed to dry to leather hardness—if quite dry it is difficult to control and if too damp sharp ridges will be made. This method is extremely attractive and something which most people love to do. White slip on a red body gives a clear outline and sharp contrast of tone under a clear glaze, with a yellow glaze both colours are softened and made warmer, with a green glaze the red will become an olive green. Some lovely Persian plates made towards the end of the 12th century have a design cut through black slip and are covered with a transparent turquoise glaze.

Slip trailing is a vigorous method of decoration which encourages simplicity by the essential speed and breadth of its execution. Trailers can be bought or made. The kind most convenient and easy to use are rubber bulbs, which are filled with slip through a funnel, and then a glass end with a narrow opening is inserted. An end can be made by inserting a quill or two quills into a cork which will fit into an old piece of inner tubing. Seventeenth century potters sometimes used the quills and cork in a pot with a narrow opening and with a hole in the side to let in air so that the flow could be controlled by the thumb over the hole. I have known potters use cows' horns too—but partly for the joy of using an unusual tool that is pleasant to handle.

Slip can be trailed directly on to the clay body, but though there are more difficulties in applying it on to a covering of wet slip there are many advantages. Dots are simplest to apply. Smaller dots of a different colour can be dropped on top of bigger dots; the dish can be tapped so that the dots flatten to level the surface. It can be tapped again until the dots flatten their sides against one another giving an attractive "biological" pattern of cells—for always a thin line of the original layer of slip will separate the dots. Or a small tilt—only a very tiny one—can give a slight elongation to each dot, or they can be feathered.

Feathering is more common when using lines. Lines are more difficult but practice soon gives control. A set of parallel lines are made across a dish, then something fine, e.g. a bristle from a brush, is pulled lightly across them at right angles. This drags one line into another but always with the thin line of the colour of the original slip covering separating them so that it gives a very fine and delicate effect. This may be done in alternate directions.

Marbling means that lines of slip are trailed on a base colour of slip, again very wet, and the mould or pot tilted and turned in different directions. Some people find this attractive, but too often it is a confession of failure.

Slip can also be fingered or combed, while still wet, through to the clay body.

One can draw with a slip trailer, and an attractive combination of line and mass is obtained by pouring slip into a dish, tilting it to get the wished-for shape, then using the trailer with another colour to draw on this shape. This has been particularly well done by William Newland on some of his strong and vigorous slip decorated plates.

Slip decorated oven dishes were in common use in England, made throughout the country in local potteries, right into the 19th century.

PHOTO: FRS

Fig. 73 Maureen's large coiled jug, painted with wax and with brown glaze poured over it.

A name particularly associated with slip decoration is that of the Toft family who worked in Staffordshire in the latter part of the 17th century and produced enormous earthenware plates. They were made of red earthenware, slipped with white and trailed in black and red under a yellowish glaze. Patterns are free and lively and include figures, birds and animals, usually with a cross-hatched border and the potter's name.

Using wax

Water and wax do not mix, so decoration utilising this fact is called wax resist. Wax is melted—ordinary candles are excellent—in a container inside a pan of water, and painted on to the pot. If the pot is then dipped in slip the slip will adhere to all the rest of the pot but run off the wax. Similarly the wax can be brushed over or painted. After a first application of colour some of the wax might be lifted and colour applied again, or wax might be painted on in a different place. If wax is applied to a biscuited pot then glaze can be used in the same way. In all cases the wax burns off in firing and unglazed portions can then be glazed with another colour or the whole pot redipped in a second glaze.

Glaze decoration

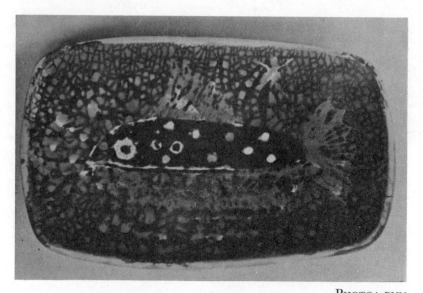

PHOTO: PMM

Fig. 74   Sheila's glaze decorated dish—white, yellow, then black superimposed.

Decoration can be done entirely by glazes. A simple form is to glaze a dish plain white. After firing cover it with a black glaze, incise into the black, then refire. This can of course be done with several colours though there is the danger of the pottery not being able to stand so many firings. A safeguard, if possible, is for each successive glaze used to have a lower maturing temperature than the preceding one. Rewards may be had—one can get all kinds of interesting effects, and unexpected ones, from glazes fired on top of one another. Just as an overfired kiln may bring lots of ruins it may also have unexpected (and unrepeatable) treasures.

If a glaze is underfired it may crackle. This in itself may be decorative but, of course, it ceases to be waterproof. However, some potters use its decorative effect and overcome this difficulty by rubbing a colour into the cracks and then refiring the glaze to its correct temperature. This can also be used when one glaze is fired on top of another, for if it is the second glaze it will tend to "take" more thickly on the cracks as there the water is absorbed more quickly.

There is also trickery of one sort or another which can be added, such as putting coloured glass marbles in specially provided hollows and channels, laying on copper wire, or making a pattern with broken pieces of coloured glass.

Combining methods

All this and others too. And any can be combined with any other. Faced with such a fantastic choice do you wonder that the mind boggles? Where to begin? That is why, in teaching, limitation is essential—in fact limitations give freedom; for given a method and a few colours there is freedom to experiment with them—given everything and a free choice is inviting muddle and preoccupation with what can be used instead of how to use it.

This has all been "HOW". Now there is "WHAT".

One certain thing is that the purpose of the decoration is to enhance the form, and whatever happens, and what is more important than anything else, is that the pattern is related to the form so that the two make one unified whole—not a pot with a pattern on it but a complete pot.

It may be that before starting to make the pot one has in mind the form complete with decoration; it may be that the method of decoration becomes apparent as the structure of the pot grows; its form or texture may already give a decorative effect which can be developed. Yet there are many times when none of these things happens, when one is faced with a built form and feels it to be incomplete without the addition of some surface decoration.

Then "WHAT". Certainly not an idea from someone else's pot—that is shame. And don't be tempted to play safe and use something tested and proved which might do—aim only for the best possible for that particular pot.

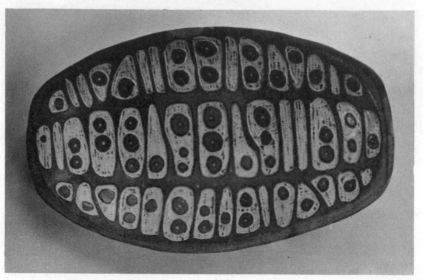

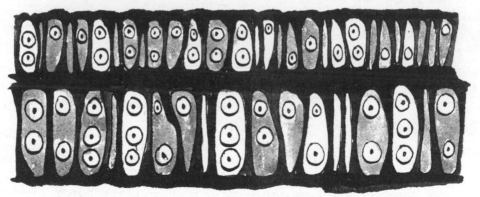

Cells. Drawing used for pattern for dish.
Note how the design is altered to fit the shape.

Fig. 75

This is when a sketchbook is more important than anything else. Do keep a sketchbook—it is more than worth its weight in gold. Lively observation is invaluable but unless recorded it is utterly lost. It is not necessary, and not particularly desirable, to have a pot in mind, or a form for use with a particular medium, when making the sketch—if it's something interesting, something which stirs the imagination, that is what matters. It may look entirely different, have a completely different effect, and give

Fig. 76 Slab bottle—pattern taken from sketches of eroded sandstone at Camber Castle, colour inlaid and painted, some areas of glaze: Mollie Winterburn.

quite a new inspiration when the original impact has faded and you leaf through the book a week or so later. Different people have different things in their sketchbooks, they are very personal, and each one will have different things which give a pattern. Mine are usually tiny things—pods and seeds, stones and shells, studies of cells, fossils, patterns on water and mud and sand, feathers, bark, raindrops, insects and eggs and caterpillars, mould, roots; sometimes very big tremendous things like erosion on a hillside, glaciers, rocks showing earth movements, and certainly forests, caves and mountains. The Natural History Museum is a wonderful place for pattern finding and everyone there is always so tolerant and kind to sketchers! Microscopic photos are useful—to actually have a microscope in the room is excellent.

Some people would get a pattern from figure groupings, some from machinery. The subject is personal but the way it is seen and used makes it into a pattern, the contrast of mass and line, of light and shade, or of smoothness and texture; to remember that curves may need the strength of a straight line or that size is scaled by contrast. And all these must be designed to emphasize the pot. Study pottery history, look at pots, learn from what has gone before, but be sincere and be an individual.

Chapter Eleven

GLAZING AND GLAZES

Glaze is a kind of glass. Just as glass can be quite transparent so can glaze, as glass can be opaque, so can glaze be thick and dense and show nothing of the surface underneath. As one can have clear, white, or different colours in glass so one can with glazes. They can also be either matt or shiny. But there is one special difference and that is that glaze must join on to the pot. If it ran when it melted as ordinary glass would, there would be a horrid shock when the kiln was opened—a pool of glaze on the kiln shelf and none on the pot! So glazes must be made so that they will stick and keep their position when they reach maturing temperature.

Purpose

Many people and many schools are unable to fire above earthenware temperature and there is probably more earthenware produced than any other type of pottery. But as everyone who has ever watered a plant in an ordinary red pot knows, earthenware is porous. Though in itself an unglazed pot or piece of ceramic sculpture is often most attractive, when intended to be a useful household utensil it must be quite waterproof, easy to keep clean, and pleasant to handle. So that is the first duty of the glaze. Another important reason for its use is to improve the appearance of the pot, so glaze is also used as a method of decoration—perhaps all over, perhaps in part, or perhaps with several glazes superimposed on one another. Although stoneware pottery vitrifies, it too is frequently glazed to make it more attractive.

Application

Bad application of glaze can ruin a pot! There are several methods, the two most common being dipping and pouring; both have their difficulties and in both speed is essential. Unless doing double dipping (a quick down-up-down movement to get the glaze inside) when glazing a pot the inside should be done first, simply and easily by pouring the glaze inside and immediately pouring it out again. The outside can then be coated either by dipping or by pouring the glaze over. Plates and dishes are more easily

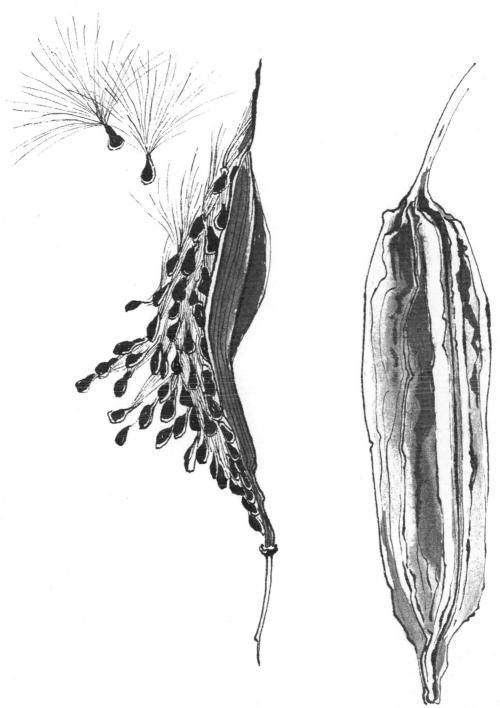

Fig. 77   From a sketchbook.

dipped, though for very large ones it may be necessary to pour. One essential is speed. One difficulty is finger marks—a place where the pot has been held so that it must be touched up with glaze and may leave an uneven patch. Where part of a pot, perhaps the foot, or part of a dish, is not to be glazed, or not to be glazed at the same time, it is easy. Otherwise the best thing is to have some longish, thin, but strong tongs to hold the pottery while it is being dipped or while glaze is poured over. The tiny specks where the tongs grip will barely show or, with many glazes, will fill in when the glaze matures. Both speed and skill will come with practice. Experience will also give knowledge of the thickness of glaze needed, for if the biscuit firing has been high the glaze can be quite thick, but if low the pots will absorb water so quickly that it needs to be much thinner. An odd piece in the firing for testing is a good thing. In low fired ware the glaze will dry almost immediately on application, but stilts should be ready on which to rest high fired ware until it is dry enough to handle.

A spray gun is a very good method of applying glaze if a very large quantity is to be done, but for individual pieces it is uneconomic—the equipment is expensive and lots of glaze is wasted.

There are other methods which are purely decorative, for example trailing the glaze just as slip is trailed. This might be done with a second colour on top of another glaze or it might be done on to the biscuit ware, and in the latter case some very interesting effects can be achieved by trailing it over a painted or inlay decoration where it will alter the colour where the two cross. A glaze can also be painted on, but, like trailing, this is a method for decoration, for brush marks will always show, the glaze will not be even, and it is difficult to get it thick enough to give it a glazed quality—some people use the glaze as a medium when painting with oxides.

There is also raw glazing. There is always more risk of cracking or distortion when applying glaze to greenware, and a further danger is that in the unlikely but possible event of one pot in the firing exploding it may leave bits sticking to other pots and ruin them too. However, if the right moment can be judged for dipping and the right glaze found to fit, then, because it has only one firing, raw glazing is much less expensive.

Making glaze

When a glaze is made the ingredients are weighed and put into a container, covered with water, mixed and sieved, first through a 60 mesh sieve to take out the coarser pieces and finally through a 120 mesh sieve, unless, as occasionally, there is a value in sieving no finer than an 80 mesh when largish specks are deliberately left in. All this is simple. The difficulty is in

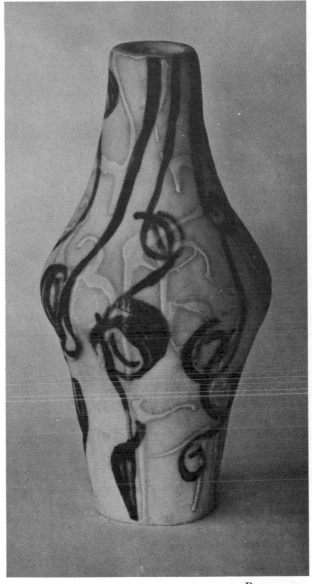

PHOTO: FRS

Fig. 78 Kathleen's pot, painted with copper and trailed with tin glaze. The pot is buff, the paint white, the copper brown on the buff but green where it is crossed by the glaze.

finding out a suitable recipe to fit the body and to get whatever qualities are wanted in the glaze.

It is, in fact, a tremendous subject—one can attend long courses of lectures or consult volume after volume full of information which, except to a very good chemist, are absolutely terrifying. Some people actually do become so fascinated by the infinite possibilities of the chemistry of glaze making that, apart from making test pieces, they have no time left to make their own pottery. At the other extreme there is the enthusiast for form, so keen on making a shape but prepared to dip it in anything to hand for a glaze. To me neither are real potters—the chemist to be much admired for skill, knowledge, inventiveness and patience; the shape builder to be pitied in not being able to complete his work himself so never able to call it really his own. For a glaze won't just "do"; like decoration it must be right for the pot.

But, to be practical, the majority of us teaching pottery are not also expert chemists and, worse, we have such limited time to teach the craft that it gives little scope to deal really thoroughly with glaze making. And first in importance is that a child should be concerned in the making of glazes so that it is not "something found in a bucket". Secondly that he should be able to get the qualities he wants. To try to achieve this I give basic recipes explaining the base—usually something containing plenty of silica; the flux—for the melting point of silica is so high that other oxides must be used to give it a lower one; and something to make it adhere to the pot, e.g. the presence of alumina will prevent the glaze running off vertical surfaces, though only a small proportion must be used. Then I give enough information for the children to be able to alter the glaze to suit their own requirements—to alter the colour, to make it more matt, to stop it running or crazing or crawling, to make it opaque or to alter the texture.

Test pieces are essential. Ours are usually quite small, to be easily found a place in the firing—perhaps 4 in. $\times$ 2 in. $\times \frac{1}{4}$ in. Biscuited a week before required, they are ready to hand—some might also be brushed with oxides to see how decoration will be affected. The test pieces and notes are the essential records. Whatever happens don't forget to put a sign on the back of the test piece—we do this in manganese. Some people, instead of notes and an identification on the test, write the whole recipe plus height and type and speed of firing on the back of the test piece. This seems laborious, but after bitter experiences of lost scraps of paper by menaces who have made a lovely glaze by some untraceable mistake perhaps it is worth it! Certainly never try out a glaze on a much loved pot before it has been thoroughly tested. When someone's experiment is successful we enter it in our glaze book—it is adopted as one of our glazes.

If for any reason one is unable to start from the basic materials, children can still be given the chance to get the effects they want, even though they have to start with a bought glaze; for they can still experiment to alter its qualities in the same ways, so that at any rate it is in part their own. The difficulty of starting with a commercial frit is that one hasn't the original recipe so more errors may be made.

PHOTO: PMM

Fig. 79   Tiny fish tile picture, shiny glazed fish contrasting matt plaster background

Kinds of glazes

When walking through a museum seeing pots which have lovely glazes made thousands of years ago just by trial and error, and the secret of making them handed down from generation to generation without any specialised knowledge of the materials or how they would behave together when fired, our task seems very simple. In fact our difficulty, as in decoration, is in having so much choice, so much technical knowledge, and such ease in getting raw materials. Early glazes were very simple and almost certainly were discovered accidentally.

Thousands of years B.C. the Egyptians were making lovely turquoise glazes with such easily obtained materials as sand, clay and soda ash.

From about 1000 B.C. lead glazes have been used in the Near East and have always been popular, for they are so practical and easy to use. Later lead glazes were used in China—they are well known on T'ang tomb sculptures. Potters in Medieval England simply sprinkled powdered galena on to their raw pottery, which produced the speckled effect, and added copper to get the green colour which is so typical. There are many advantages in lead glazes—they are easily made matt by the addition of a little alumina, they have a very wide firing range, and it is also possible to obtain a wide colour range. There are disadvantages too, one particular one being that lead is poisonous and its use in any raw form forbidden except to the individual. However lead frits are easily obtained, the most useful being lead bisilicate and lead sesquisilicate, for when lead oxide is fritted with enough quantities of other oxides it becomes non-poisonous; so these we can use.

Lots of early Chinese pots we see have uneven glaze, perhaps only on one side or a shoulder, so ash glazes too are generally thought to have been discovered accidentally by ashes from wood fires being blown through a kiln. Materials are very simple—any wood or vegetable ash, some felspar and some clay; the difficulty is that a high temperature is necessary to mature these. That is why for many years only the Chinese used them, for only they had kilns which could achieve sufficient heat.

Alkaline glazes, which use sodium or potassium for a flux, are very popular with some people because brilliant strong colours can be made, turquoises from copper, vivid blues from cobalt, and deep browns and purples with iron and manganese. However, there are certain disadvantages, especially that they very easily run if at all overfired; they also are apt to craze, and as they are rather soft they scratch easily.

Colour in glazes

Colour in glazes is normally obtained by the addition of metal oxides. These must be added when the glaze is made, for they are calculated as percentages of the dry weight of the other ingredients.

Iron, usually added as ferric oxide, gives yellows and browns using from 1–7%, though colour varies too according to the other ingredients. Iron is also very useful for using with other oxides in order to modify their brightness and give more subtle colours. Iron chromate gives greys.

Manganese gives purple browns and richer browns with iron. Like cobalt it will give specks if not well ground. In lead glazes it seems apt to blister if there is more than 8%.

Copper is usually added as copper carbonate or black copper oxide. Not more than 4% should be used, for larger amounts tend to give a metallic black, but normally with lead it gives greens and with alkaline glazes turquoises. In reduction firing it gives a lovely red; this, because copper escapes at a high temperature, causing lovely red patches on pots.

Chrome oxide I personally usually avoid, for while it will normally give a dark green it may also give yellow or a nasty pink due to the presence of other things in the kiln such as soda or tin.

Small amounts of nickel, less than 1% give pleasant greys but 2% or more give browns.

Cobalt always gives blues. It is a very strong colour and even 0.2% will give a good blue and 1% a dark blue. Unless extremely well ground it will be mottled. The strong colour can be made more interesting by adding other oxides such as iron, manganese, or nickel, and underglaze yellow added will give a very pleasant colour.

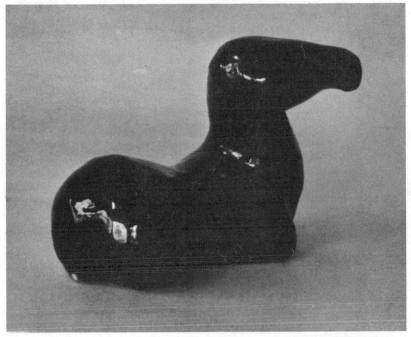

Fig. 80   Sue's horse. Olive green glaze on red clay.

Matt quality

Very smooth shiny pots are certainly practical. There are no crevices so they are very hygienic and very easy to keep clean, but this glossiness has a cheap, gaudy, unattractive look. When a glaze is matt it means in most cases that it is not completely melted and has a slightly rough surface, and this is much more pleasing, especially when it is not completely opaque and metal oxides break through. This can usually be achieved by adding more clay, alumina, or whiting—though not the last if the glaze is fired above $1075°C$, for then the whiting becomes a flux. Remember not to let the kiln cool too quickly, for this will make the glaze shiny.

Crazing (pings) might be due to one of the following: taking out of the kiln too soon, the kiln having cooled too quickly, the biscuit having been underfired or the glaze having been underfired—any of these are easily corrected.

Experiment! It is a good idea to read books about glazes and find out as much as possible, and to see what other people are doing and find out how they do it; but easily the most important thing is to try it out for oneself—to use one's own materials on one's own clay body—to try adding a little of this or that and see what happens, to try it over oxides or over another glaze. Keep records—it is surprising how quickly a personal reference library of test pieces will build up.

APPENDIX

Usually no potter likes to tell another potter a glaze recipe, not because of being secretive or wanting to keep a good thing to himself, but because only too often it doesn't work for someone else—there are so many small things about the clay body or the firing and the mixing, or other ingredients in the kiln, which make a big difference to the quality of the glaze, so that the result may not be the same for any two people.

However, here are a few suggestions for starting points:

Either	A.	Lead Bisilicate	70 parts
		Cornish Stone	20 parts
		China Clay	10 parts
or	B.	Lead sesquisilicate	53 parts
		Felspar	32 parts
		Whiting	7 parts
		China Clay	5 parts
		Flint	3 parts

make a good glaze and have the typically wide firing range of lead glazes. Normally I would fire these between 1080°C and 1120°C. Try adding things to these to alter the opacity or colour. For example, 10 parts tin oxide added to A will give a white glaze. Another 0.2 of titanium will give a white glaze of slightly different quality. Add tiny quantities of alumina or perhaps some stoneware clay or finely ground grog and it may be less shiny.

To B another 7 parts tin, 2 parts titanium and 1 part zinc will also give a white glaze—this one a very dense white. Two or 3 parts ferric oxide added to B will give a deep honey colour, very pleasant over white slip on red. Three parts copper carbonate to B gives a green which is a very pleasant olive on red clay; on buff clay it is a typical copper green through which oxides will show, but it is a little dark for use with slip. Three parts manganese, 2 cobalt, 1 copper and 1 iron will give a dense shiny black.

A more pleasant black is obtained by

Lead Bisilicate	61 parts
China Clay	20 parts
Cornish Stone	9 parts
Whiting	5 parts
Manganese	7 parts

This is brownish on buff clay, quite black on red, and if not fired above 1080°C has a lovely dull shine—fired higher it is too shiny.

If the brightness of alkaline glazes is wanted, why not try an alkaline frit and add different quantities of copper and cobalt, perhaps trying a little iron or underglaze yellow mixed with them? We have a delightful colourful set of test pieces from doing just this.

If able to fire to stoneware, then:

Felspar	48
China Clay	22
Whiting	20
Flint	10

is a good base from which to start.

If able to fire ash glazes then they are the simplest and most delightful of all, just made by ash, clay and felspar, perhaps a little flint or whiting being used as well. A good proportion to try, in order to get a start, is equal proportions of ash and felspar and only half as much clay. Of course unless prepared to burn wood so carefully as to get ash of only one type, do not expect results to be exactly repeated with each batch of glaze!

Chapter Twelve

KILNS AND FIRING

A kiln is the one absolutely essential piece of apparatus needed to make pottery. These can vary between an expensive, modern electric kiln which controls rise and fall of temperature and has a pyrometer and reduction elements; and a tiny one-pot upturned flowerpot kiln heated by a fire in a trench dug in the ground underneath, with an updraught to the hole in the top. Though it is very important to have an efficient reliable kiln to produce pottery without an unnecessary waste of time and materials, yet there is one very good reason why primitive kilns should not be despised and why in schools, every so often, one should be made and used. This is that firing can be so much more easily understood if seen and if the fire is made and lit and if the amount of heat and speed of firing are controlled. So though I would not recommend them for constant everyday use here are two very simple methods of firing; they will not reach a very high temperature and they will make a lot of work, but the results may well be worth it.

Sawdust kiln

Round a slight hollow in the ground build a wall of bricks. A rectangular shape is the easiest. Leave small spaces in the brickwork, for these will help the fire. Cover the bottom with sawdust four to six inches deep, put in the heaviest pots to be fired, fill with sawdust and cover with another four inches of sawdust. Then the next heaviest pots and so on to the top, and then leave a thick layer; for there the fire is lit and the heat must not be too sudden. Paper will be needed to help the fire start, but once going it must be controlled immediately, for it is essential that it burns very very slowly. It will need watching at first but eventually can be left. Cover with a piece of corrugated iron with holes in for the smoke to escape—not too many or it will quicken the firing. If burning too quickly add more sawdust at once. The common fault with sawdust kilns is too quick firing —it should take at least twelve hours, and should also be allowed to cool equally slowly. Quick firing will lead to cracked pots. There is no need to spread wire netting across from side to side to prevent pots falling down on one another—it is better that they should sink down with the fire, and with the precaution of the heaviest being on the bottom, breakages are rare—normally the pots are found next day comfortably cushioned in ash.

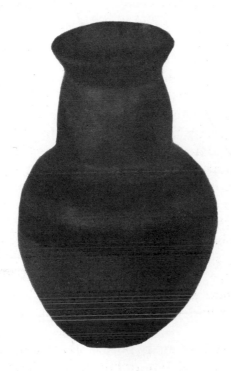

Fig. 81   A Ndondo from Barotseland, showing smoke marks from firing in an open fire.

Peat kiln

This is my favourite primitive kiln, but one is not necessarily in a part of the country where a supply of peat can easily be obtained! Cut away the turf in a circle of about one yard in diameter, scoop out a hollow, and lay a fire; lining the hollow with small stones if it is damp. Start the fire with anything that will burn easily, and gradually add sticks to form a small cone. When they are burning cover with peat, leaving a small hole at the top for smoke to escape, and on this covering layer of peat place the pots with peat round and inside them. Then another complete layer of peat, then pots, until a low cone is built, and finally replace the turf on top, for this will slow the burning. The peat insulates the pots from the sudden fierce heat of the burning sticks and by its slow burning will heat up the pots before it begins to burn round them. Firing may take up to 48 hours and should not take less than 12. The pots will be a lovely black from contact with the peat and lack of air.

Other methods of heating

Making and using one of these primitive kilns will show that firing must be controlled so that the temperature rises slowly and that there is not only sufficient heat but sufficient time for the chemical changes to take place to turn greenware (pottery before firing) into pottery. These principles are the same whatever the fuel of the kiln and that is a matter of personal choice and, to a large extent, the siting of the kiln.

I have been in a lovely country pottery where I was astonished to find the kiln fired with coal and was assured that this was the cheapest and the best for that particular kiln. It took two or three days to fire, had several fire mouths, and was very hard work, but since it was so very large it was only fired four times a year.

Wood is a wonderful fuel for kilns and gets lovely results, but unless one has one's own supply it is very expensive, and it also involves an extra lot of hard work cutting it up and in stoking—as wood burns quickly it is hard work to keep up. Michael Cardew had a wood-fired kiln in Abuja in Northern Nigeria where he has done wonderful work introducing the wheel, glaze and high firing and yet somehow keeping the feel of the local traditional pottery.

Oil firing is favoured by many potters as very much cheaper and it also reaches high temperatures, but technical knowledge is necessary. One of the most successfully built kilns I have seen (Farnham Art School) combined both wood and oil firing so that it gets both the exciting effects and the high firing.

Coke is favoured by some people who do something akin to raku firing, for once going coke can reach a high temperature quite quickly. An open-work rectangular brick-built structure, with holes to let in air and for riddling ash, has a fire of wood and coal laid in it with a saggar with the pots in the centre. When the fire is going coke is added and this makes a lovely red hot glowing fire. Eager peeps show when the glaze has melted, the lid is pushed to one side and the pots taken out with tongs and dropped into a bath of cold water. There is a hiss and a cloud of steam and the pots can be handled at once. This is fun. Why they are not in fragments I can't imagine!

Gas is very good and many people's favourite. Very high temperatures can be reached and reduction firing is not difficult.

Electric kilns are also very good and very reliable. Certainly it is not so easy to do a reduction firing, but there is less difficulty about siting than with a gas kiln, they do not need a special chimney, and they are extremely easy to manage. They have the advantage of controlled even heating and need less attention than any other kind of kiln. They seem to stand up well to hard work—the one in the school where I teach has been in constant heavy use and is always fired twice a week, sometimes three times, yet very occasional renewal of an element has been the only expense in seven years.

Kiln furniture

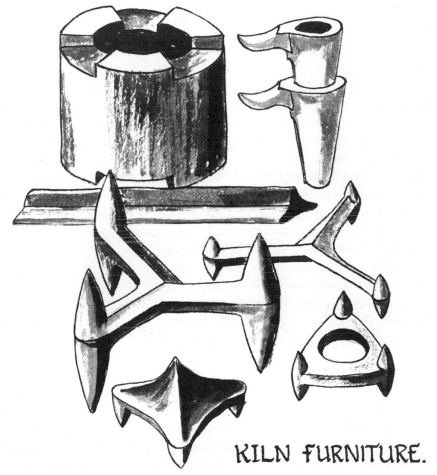

KILN FURNITURE.
Prop, thimble, saddle, spur, and various stilts.

Fig. 82

This consists of kiln shelves on which the pottery stands and props which support the shelves. Both are usually made of silimanite, which will stand a very high temperature. Shelves can be obtained in a large variety of size, shape and thickness; and props in two or three sizes which will fit together to make whatever height is wanted. No other furniture is needed for a biscuit firing, but when pots arc covered with glaze then they must stand away from the shelf and a variety of supports is available to suit the size or shape of the pieces being fired. These consist mainly of stilts of various kinds and sizes, usually supporting the pot in three places. Saddles are long triangular pieces—very useful for the odd shapes one may get with modelled or multiple forms. Spurs have only one point and are very useful where an extra support is needed or when something stands on three or four asymmetrically arranged feet.

Packing

One may have no choice in packing arrangements because of awkward sizes and shapes of certain articles. This is expensive in firing space but well worth it for special things. Generally it is a good idea to group pieces of about the same height together to use space to its best advantage. If it is an electric kiln make sure pots are not too close to the elements—it is wise to have a good half inch to an inch clearance of the shelves from the sides. Props are best under one another—if, near the top, a small shelf is used part way on top of another so that a prop is inevitably in the middle where there are no props underneath, then less heavy things are best on this. Actually shelves rarely crack, but if there is a sign of one then it is safer not to use it—two small pieces may be useful sometime. In a biscuit firing pots can just touch, so could be fired on top of one another providing that they touch rim to rim. Also they could be on sand inside one another —the top one being the lightest, and taking care that they cannot lock. Naturally always start packing at the back and fill one layer before starting on the one above so that space can be clearly seen. If it is a glost firing handle carefully and never touch the rims of the pots, for that is where glaze flakes off most easily. On no account must pots in a glost firing touch one another or any part of the kiln or kiln furniture. If there is danger of thick glaze running off a pot when it melts, put a little sand underneath and, when unpacking, if anything like this has happened, clean it off, and any other bits on shelves or props, straight away, for it is a nuisance to find furniture not ready for use when repacking. In a stoneware firing use no stilts, for the body may wilt over them—just see that the glaze comes no lower than $\frac{1}{4}$ in. from the bottom.

Measuring the heat

Some very experienced potters may really know the temperature of their kiln by the colour, but this ability is rare and certainly not for any but the expert. The best method of measuring heat is by seger cones. These are made of pottery mixtures which will melt at given temperatures, for example, an 01A cone will melt at 1080°C. When it has bent right over so that the top is level with the bottom, it is ready. Three cones differing by 20° used together are useful—the middle one being the correct temperature. The first gives an indication of when the second will be ready, the third tells if the kiln should go beyond the temperature required. The easiest thing to use is a pyrometer, for its reading simply gives the temperature of the kiln at any time; however the cones are most reliable for they show the state of the pots. If cones are used they must be placed so that they can be clearly seen through one of the spy holes. Often it is inconvenient to place a cone in such a position and on occasions the space cannot be spared; then one must depend on the pyrometer. It is a good thing to check on the pyrometer readings with cones sometimes, and also to place cones in various parts of the kiln to find out if the temperature varies between top and bottom or back and front. Potters used to use small rings of clay to find out the state of their pottery—these were put where they could be hooked out for testing.

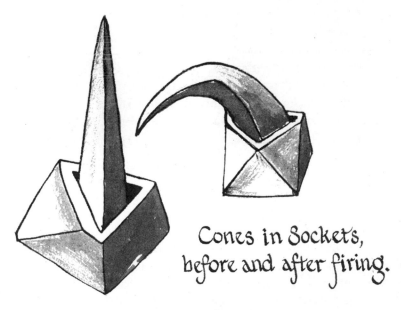

Cones in Sockets, before and after firing.

Fig. 83

Firing
When the pots are formed and dried, but are still clay, they are called greenware. This is put into the kiln for its first firing, the biscuit firing,

133

when it undergoes chemical changes so that it becomes pottery. This is called biscuit ware. If it is then covered with glaze and put into the kiln again, this is called a glost firing and the pottery taken out is glazed pottery. This latter firing is normally oxidised and, like ordinary burning, it takes place combining with oxygen from the air. If the air supply is cut down then the fire, needing oxygen, will take it from the colours and glazes in the kiln. This changes them and so gives certain colour qualities and glaze qualities not otherwise obtainable; for example, that is how red is obtained from copper, and how blue and green are obtained from iron. Reduction is only temporarily necessary, so the firing both starts and finishes as an ordinary oxidised firing but is reduced just before the glaze melts and intermittently afterwards, not for more than half an hour at a time because it causes a slight drop in temperature. One can get this effect by almost closing off the air; by burning something in the kiln to consume the oxygen; or by stoking with so much fuel that it cannot all burn—according to the kind of kiln one has.

It is very important that a firing should begin very slowly, especially if it is a biscuit firing. Where possible, with kilns in schools, it is a good plan to fill the kiln, leave it on very low all night, and bring up the heat until the right temperature is reached next day. With an electric kiln this is very easy—I would suggest it goes on a low heat all night (30), is brought up to a medium heat next morning (70) for about an hour, then full heat and turn on the bottom elements too, and the firing should be complete soon after midday. Never open the kiln too soon. If it is a biscuit firing it might be possible to open it next day, but it will be too soon for glost. To avoid temptation I usually pack and fire a biscuit kiln at the beginning of the week and a glost at the end. The weekend ensures that it won't be opened too soon!

Earthenware, stoneware, and porcelain

These are really terms which relate to the height of firing of a piece of pottery and thus to its hardness. Earthenware is the softest and a usual temperature for earthenware is about 1100°C. Stoneware might be fired between 1250°C and to over 1300°C, and porcelain from 1300°C upwards; the highest of all being industrial porcelain. Earthenware is porous and needs glaze to be waterproof. Stoneware is vitrified. Certain clays will not stand high temperatures and will wilt if fired too high, so it is necessary to find this out if wanting to make stoneware and if necessary to experiment with the clay body.

Most of the pottery in the world is earthenware, and much throughout all periods of history is lovely. This is because earthenware clays are the most commonly found and earthenware temperatures the easiest to attain.

Fig. 84   Stoneware slab built bottles (Mollie Winterburn). Patterns from tattered leaf and yew tree trunk.

For school use earthenware is ideal; it is excellent for terracotta models and very good to use for an understanding of pottery technique. One of its firings ought to go up to about 1100°C. It seems to be a matter of personal preference which it is. In industry it appears to be general to have a high biscuit firing and a lower glost, but most schools and colleges use a lower biscuit firing—perhaps only 1020°–1040°C—and a higher glost. I certainly find the latter easiest, for it is much more difficult to apply glazes to higher fired ware.

Chapter Thirteen

PROJECTS

Pottery is no exception to group work. For many reasons it is a good idea to sometimes work together on one project and, as in other subjects, individual contributions will vary. In this subject this factor is a great help. Those who have the greater intelligence and ability are soon in charge of the planning and building, and yet everyone takes pride in their own individual bit and is easily made to feel that without their piece it will not be complete. It is also a means of both enriching the school and of having work seen, for not only can large projects become part of the school but there is no desire (as with everything else immediately it is finished!) to take them home. So here are a few suggestions of things which have proved quite good things to do.

Fig. 85

Fig. 86   Animal pot.

Big coil pots

Perhaps like me you find it difficult to have many large pots being made at the same time because of sheer lack of space—this being intensified by the fact that made by one child with one short lesson a week many large pieces need storage for a very long time.

The pot in Fig. 86 was made in two lessons by one form; incidentally with great enthusiasm. The clay is grogged and sanded and it is about twenty inches high. The idea was animals going to the pond to drink, and the shape and placing of the lugs planned first. The banding wheel was in the centre of the room. Someone rolled the base. Those who preferred to coil made the coils and those who preferred to model made the animals. Coils were added as they were made by each child, but as the pot grew two skilled builders controlled the form, this being completed in the first lesson. During the week both pot and animals were allowed to harden just a little so that in the second lesson the shoulder of the pot was stiff enough to take the animals and both could be scraped and neatened where necessary. The differences in choice and of treatment also add interest and liveliness.

Tile panels

Very large tile panels also take a very long time for one individual to make in short lessons, but made by a group are again something useful made in only two or three lessons.

Themes connected with the school or other building, offering a wall to be decorated in this way, are obviously ideal, and those using birds, fish, animals, insects, flowers—anything which can be made individually but with great variety—are useful, as are also pieces which make units of a whole. The variation in size which is a natural result of work by separate individuals becomes an asset; some will work boldly on a large scale, some minutely and in detail, and both will have a place in the complete panel. The differences in choice and of treatment also add interest and liveliness. There must inevitably be many pieces which are discarded, but if each child has made several then there is more likelihood of at any rate one of them fitting in harmoniously and no one being hurt. The great danger of getting pieces which will not make a unified composition can be met in various ways—a simple colour scheme or one certain method of decoration are obvious examples.

Tile pictures which are flat can make decorative table tops for a recreation room. Perhaps a new floor is needed in a porch or alcove—smallish pieces set in cement or concrete will wear well.

Fig. 87 Decorative bricks.

Walls

Why not make a real wall—not just the decoration on it? Perhaps a piece of garden could be sheltered by a low decorative wall. Or perhaps a section of classroom could be walled off—I like to keep a separate section in the pottery for the use of books for reading and sketching.

When the city of Babylon became the capital of a new dynasty in the third millenium B.C. there were many innovations in building and clay was one of the few materials in abundant supply. All the principal public buildings were on one wide street which led right across the town to the temple. Where it went through the city wall was a great gateway—the Ishtar Gate. To those who went along to the palace of Nebuchadnezzar it must have made a vivid impression, for the walls, the great gate, and the public buildings were made of glazed bricks in bright colours. On a deep blue background standing in relief in whites and yellows were animals; some recognisable, bulls, oxen and lions; and others mythical. Geometric patterns framed the gate and edged the walls, these also being brilliant in blue and turquoise, white and yellow.

Each huge individual animal was built up on a thick panel of clay so that it stood out in relief from its background, and before the clay went hard the whole panel was cut across and across into separate bricks. These were fired and glazed and the figure put together again when the wall was built. They have proved astonishingly durable—one visitor is known to have said that the angles are still so clear and sharp and the colours so good that they might have been taken out of the kiln yesterday and not almost four thousand years ago.

The bricks in Fig. 87 were made by some fourteen-year-old girls as a preliminary experiment. The intention is to make a low wall to surround a section of garden. The lower part will be of solid brick and these decorative pierced bricks will make a border, inset alternately with solid bricks for stability and with one row of solid bricks above.

Belts, bracelets and necklaces

I include these almost with shame—yet they give delight to many girls, and perhaps it is a relief after something very large and strong to make something tiny and delicate. Like all things they can be made very well or very badly. Certainly towards the end of term with shelves of big unfired pieces queueing for a place in the one overworked kiln it is with a feeling of thankfulness that one sees an absorbed group patiently perfecting the fit of small exquisite shapes which will hang together. There is a certain craftiness on the other side too—teacher will almost certainly say that anything big must wait till next term to be fired, but little pieces will fit in anywhere—they can be slipped into another pot, under the curve of a dish, in all sorts of odd corners where nothing else will go.

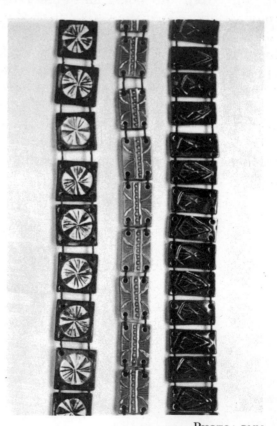

PHOTO: PMM

Fig. 88   Belts made by Dorothy, Gwenda and Pat.

PHOTO: PMM

Fig. 89   Mobile pieces based on seedcases, waiting for selection.

Mobiles

Pottery mobiles are rather heavier than most and are not likely to be swung by the breeze! But even if they need a push to start them moving they can certainly be mobile. The whole thing can be done as a ceramic with pieces hanging from odd shapes which may look like pottery coathangers or wheels, but it seems sensible to combine wire in their building, for not only is it easier to make something which will twist, but it is less fragile. Cautiously we tried first with flat abstract shapes with an arrangement of holes in an effort to keep weight to a minimum; but far more appealing to a child was to discover (on a museum visit) tiny Greek toys, some being little birds with a hole through, obviously meant to hang and swing on a cord. This was a lovely subject but restraint in flight was necessary to avoid tangles.

Seed pods again became a direct inspiration, many having holes—and simplified shapes patted from pinch pots, carefully hollowed, with the holes making an important part of the decoration, gave delightful and varied light hanging shapes.

143

Lighting

A wide variety of work is possible in relation to lighting. Making lamp bases has become very commercialised; yet much more interesting work can be done than the rather standardised ones we see, and more subtle use can be made of the light if the entire lamp is planned in clay. Holes are especially valuable; the light can be made to show through them in patterns, by careful use of angles it can be deflected and directed, and by glaze and shape the container can either be a brilliant reflector of light, or it can screen it and give only a glow of light.

Fig. 90 shows a large standing lamp with no direct light—light comes from the top and through the holes in the neck, the latter being cut at varying angles and forming a pattern of light on the shoulder of the pot.

Candle holders for an evening meal give enormous scope. They can be single or grouped, or made to be regrouped, they can be of varying height, they can be arranged with a pattern to give out light, or to form a pattern with shadows.

Wall electric lights are very popular and can be made with unobtrusive holes in the back for screwing to the wall. Glaze can be craftily used—a really high gloss one has a place here, for it can reflect and intensify light inside the container with perhaps a network of cut shapes, like some Persian vases, on the outer part.

Night lights have a rather stronger light than candles and are excellent for just this kind of decorative light for which play with shape is ideal. They can be made as hanging containers or, less conventionally but perhaps more usefully, with a flattish base for standing on a table and a perforated cover to place over.

One thing to remember is that lights to hang should be as light in weight as possible, while those to stand are actually better on the heavy side to avoid the danger of being knocked over.

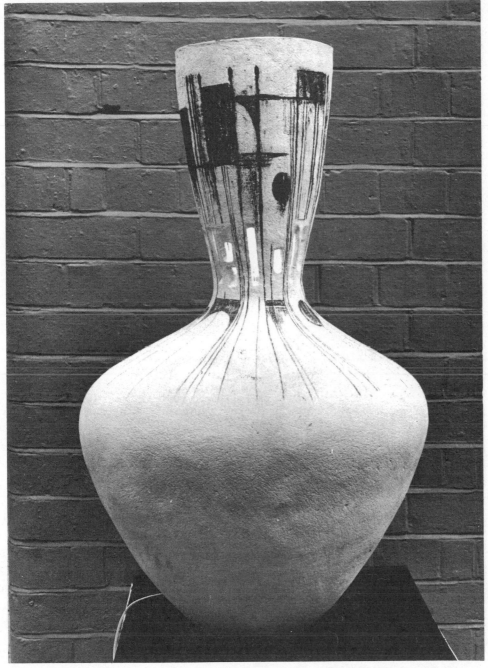

Fig. 90   Lamp: Mollie Winterburn.

PHOTO: PMM

Fig. 91   Spindles.

Combining crafts

No one wants to be cut off and narrowed down to their own little corner. Obviously people will always have scope for seeing other work, trying other crafts, and applying ideas from one to another. Just as pottery cannot be separated from sculpture, so the enormous value of drawing can never, never be underestimated in a pottery; the use of painting is obvious, and certain things, if their use is not immediately apparent, can be deliberately made as a link between crafts. Spindle whorls are ideal; they need care and thought in making, can be very decorative, and can be used afterwards in the weaving room. Loom weights too. If lamps are designed to have the base only made in pottery with a related shape and size in mind for the shade, this might be covered with a woven material or perhaps with something gathered such as reeds held securely by woven threads. Because they were so attractive I have used reeds with flowers, expecting them to drop in a week or two—but finding them still entire after three years we've been encouraged to weave other decorative grasses into shades. They have not all been successful, some drop and are a nuisance but others keep and it is worth finding these out.

146

Fig. 92 Bottles: Mollie Winterburn. Odd pieces of lino left over by a class making lino blocks for fabric printing were cut up and pressed in. The pattern is derived from the Franks Casket.

A lamp base might be designed specifically to suit a piece of hand-printed fabric, a dish to take a curved cane handle for lifting; or a pot to have an arrangement of cane or woven cords for hanging.

Lino is useful. Patterns can be put on to clay using lino just as they can with potato cuts, but another thing we like is to collect the odd pieces of lino, cut off and unwanted pieces, and use these to press into soft clay. The pattern of the one in Fig. 92 derives from the Franks Casket!

Carving clay

If you ever get clay delivered with the packets inadvertently broken open during transit you have the problem of lumps of hard dry clay. The normal thing is to break it up into tiny lumps, soak it, and get it ready for pugging. Yet there are people who want to use it as it is, who have a feeling for sculpture rather than pottery, who prefer to carve down to a shape rather than build one up. These hard lumps are ideal for them, for usually it is clay straight from a pug mill with few if any airholes or impurities. Once faced with this problem on a large scale, I fired many carved figures and shapes, some as much as five inches thick, of which none exploded and only one or two had very slight cracks.

Plantholders

The green of foliage looks well with the reds of secondary clays. Containers for plants can be single or multiple, they can be made for house or garden, they can be made to rest on a table, to fit a windowsill, to stand on the floor, to hang on the walls, to stand among other plants or on concrete outside. A point to remember, if they are for indoors, is that plants must be watered, so that the design must include something to protect the part which will touch wall or furniture. A tray or tiling may be made to fit a windowsill, a base glazed inside for the table, and for pots hanging on walls I have often found a "fin" is sufficient.

Fig. 93   Hard clay, carved, polished and biscuit fired. Nora Gibbs.

Garden sculpture

This is a pretentious title but it covers all kinds of things—none of them gnomes or toadstools! There are all kinds of things which can be attractive as well as useful, or there can actually be ceramic sculpture. The sketch, Fig. 94, is a plan for a sort of bird totem pole. It's not designed in any detail and it is not merely possible but very probable that it will alter during construction. This is a good thing for, firstly, however good the drawing, a child does not get from it an immediate conception in three dimensions; secondly were it too complete and final it would leave no room for creation during making—which is a desirable thing as one meets the problems of building.

Fig. 94   Birds, planned as ceramic, carried out in cold cast metal by senior girls.

Birds like baths and food tables. Different sized baths are pleasing to design but remember to make them all shallow. The one photographed (95) has baths (and a diving board!), perches which can be stuck in the holes when required, a place for food and a place for a plant. It has its faults—the shelf for food is above a bath and those untidy careless birds will drop their crumbs in the water! Next time the food table will be at the very bottom! But the two top baths are very well patronised. Some birds like food which hangs and this is a little low for them, so they are tempted by little containers hanging in the trees. A nesting box has so far proved unacceptable.

Fig. 95   Bird bath: Mollie Winterburn.

PHOTO: PMM

Fig. 96   Coiled figures.

This group of figures (96) was made by three fifteen-year-old girls to stand out of doors.

Fountains have lots of possibilities. All kinds of shapes which can have thin pipes for water inserted can be designed to shoot water into the air, singly or in groups, and jets can be designed so that they fall over certain shapes or into hollows, from which they might gradually cascade downwards, or by which they could be made to change direction and have an interesting ground plan.

Musical instruments

Really inventive people can design all kinds of things to make sounds. We have only tried whistles, bells and drums. Whistle making is described fully in Chapter Two, and many different tones and notes can be obtained. Pottery would seem to be the most unsuitable material possible for a bell and sound is not very good, but it is feasible and the bells are much more durable than one would imagine.

Fig. 97   Drums, coiled, made by fourteen-year-old girls.

Drums are excellent, and, as with the whistles, size and shape alter the sound. As there is almost unlimited choice in form and in decoration they are a most satisfactory subject and they can be made to stand, to hold, or to hang—the last being another good opportunity of combining work with the weaving department. The set of drums illustrated was made by a third year form, a group of fourteen-year-old girls. All are coiled.

Roof finials

Birds in silhouette against the sky along the house block roof

Fig. 98

Glazed pottery used to be used extensively in China both as roof tiles and as architectural ornaments. Roofs, being the most prominent and characteristic feature of Chinese architecture, were often glowing with colour, with delightful glazed tiling, specially decorated tiles for the lowest in each row, specially shaped tiles for the ridges, and very special end tiles, perhaps with a dragon turning inwards. These glazed terracottas were actually made as part of the ridge tile—sometimes there would be whole rows of animals. Yellow was a popular colour, not that anyone could dare select the colour of the tiles of their roof, or of the decorations in the house, these matters were fixed according to their station in life—just as the dragon has five claws on wares for the emperor, four for princes, and three for any-

Figs. 99 and 100 Birds for the roof project.

one else, so the colour of roof tiles was used to distinguish a palace of the emperor, the residence of a noble, or one of the state temples.

The birds in Figs. 99 and 100 have been made to stand along the edge of the roof of one of our house blocks so that the shapes will stand out against the sky. They are all coiled and glazed and intended to be cemented in place. The average height is twenty inches, large enough to be seen, but not too large as this is only a one-storey building. Many girls have taken part in their making.

Fig. 101 Francine's lamp—pottery base and woven shade.

These are just a few of my own ideas which we have carried out. Everyone else will have heaps of different ideas and lots of interesting work is possible.

Chapter Fourteen

POTS AND POTTERS

Sometimes one gets a thrill not from a rock formation, seed or strange growth, but quite directly from the work of some other potter. It may be an anonymous one from the past or a friend in the next village. This is not a desire to copy their shapes or patterns but a starting point for something quite different. Perhaps it is an understanding of the motive which has led in that direction and gives a sudden insight into how it can be taken further, carried on in another direction, or re-translated.

Pottery history

A knowledge of pottery history is invaluable and courses of study are easy to arrange and are a matter of individual preference. To do this by certain periods and places is the easy way but is apt to be narrow and gives little scope for individual interests. But certainly it is very valuable to have a background of knowledge to which to relate personal studies. I try to give first information about the pottery made at different periods in this country, for example, the Neolithic, the Roman, the Saxon, the Medieval, 17th century slipware, etc., which not only easily fall into place through the history lessons but are also a guide when pottery sherds are found or collected. There must obviously also be an introduction to certain great periods in pottery making—to select at random—perhaps the Islamic, the Han and Sung, the Hispano Moresque, the Greek and the Corean. In addition, all things taught in making and doing will have been related to pottery of the past—inevitably, prehistoric when teaching coiling, Japanese when making slabs, perhaps Chinese climbing kilns when discussing firing, Sung plates when incising, the Tofts when slipping, bellarmines when thinking of salt glazing, majolica when using tin glazes, and so on.

But it is the bringing about of the desire for personal study which is of far the greatest importance. With a general background and a knowledge of how to make notes and sketches, then work can develop. There are many ways of giving initial impetus and after that it is only individual help which is needed. I am always astonished to find out children's different enthusiasms. One liked an octopus pattern on a Minoan pot, she found other octopuses on other pots, found out a great deal about Mediterranean pottery and also about Greek trade routes and colonies. Another developed a love for Mochica and Nasca pottery and judging by her notebook must have spent many absorbed hours in the Ethnological Department of the British Museum. More traditionally, one chose brushwork on Far Eastern pottery, but also became proficient herself; while her friend tried to get the feel of the strength and solidity of Medieval wares. A history of tile making gave a very wide field of study, so too did one of animal lugs and handles.

Starting points have varied enormously. Perhaps it has only been a visit to a museum—it is extraordinary how children will not visit one until they have been taken, after which they find their way with surprising ease. Setting a problem is a good starting point too, e.g., ways of joining two pots together, different ways of designing handles for lifting, carrying, or hanging; or perhaps just finding examples of certain types of decoration.

Following up a find always arouses enthusiasm, and somehow, when there is interest, things come. I have had incised and combed sherds of Roman coarse ware and pieces of mortaria with the potter's stamp pressed in, both from the foundations of a new housing estate, and been able to get permission for keener children to be allowed to help with the "dig". A nearly complete 17th century Tickenhall ware vase dredged up from the bottom of a river was brought home by someone's Dad in his "snap tin". An 18th century ink bottle was found in a hole in the road. All these caused a "want to know more about it" feeling.

Potters
Seeing someone actually "doing it" is perhaps even more thrilling and although it usually means a lot of time and trouble to arrange a visit its value makes it worthwhile. Unfortunately country potteries are becoming fewer and fewer, but there are still some where the owners are kind enough to have school parties on certain days and show the source of the clay supply, how it is made usable, the kind of things they make, and their kilns—all of which are so much better remembered and understood through having been actually seen. If in the vicinity of a factory a visit there will give a very different but also valuable experience. A visit to a studio potter is not so easy; it would be unjust to ask a single person working alone to afford the time, for even with the great interest in pottery today it is difficult to earn a living and keep a soul! However, keen children will always find someone who will let them visit and tell them about their work. Then there are exhibitions of an individual potter's work or of the work of a pottery. Admittedly this is much easier in London but there are such exhibitions available, though less frequently, within reach of most people. The older girls I teach have been extremely lucky in visiting exhibitions and actually

Fig.   *Corked bottles: Mollie Winterburn. The animals were made with "drawing pin" bases*
to push and glue into the corks.

meeting the potter who has on every occasion been very kind, told them
about the work and answered innumerable questions. Then there are the
mixed exhibitions such as those at the Craftsmen Potters' Shop (3 Lowndes
Court, Carnaby Street, London, W.1) and the Crafts Centre (Hay Hill,
Berkeley Street, London, W.1).

Illustrations

Keeping illustrations takes a lot of time but having things for reference is valuable. When starting this seems a simple job, just a pile for handbuilt ones, one for commercial ones and one for historical ones; but in a very short while classification becomes extremely difficult. Now I seem to have sets for method—pinch, coil, tile, mosaic, dish, slab, thrown and slip cast, modelling and pottery with modelling, and pottery made by mixed methods, shapes which are joined together, and groups of pottery. Then there are sheets of pottery from different historical periods, lots and lots of them, also sheets of the work of well-known potters and potteries. After this are pages showing different methods of decoration, different textures, and perhaps groups of subjects such as drums or jugs to show how differently they can be treated. Finally, and a copious section, are things which help to suggest pattern—photographs of birds and flowers and seeds and trees, of fields; and rocks and mud and sand and water; of ships and buildings, and of animals, insects and fish. These are made available, together with books, in a part of the room where clay is not used.

Records of work

Naturally people want their pots. Work is kept for a time so that there is always something to show in the pottery and something to set a standard, but eventually it goes home. It's nice to know what has been made and to remember the people who did it. It is expensive but pleasant to have a photographic record of the better and the more exciting work done. There may be a camera club or someone who is interested. Slides are excellent and can be used for talks too, and children love to see their own and their friends' pots appearing on the screen.

MATERIALS AND SUPPLIERS

Various materials and tools have been mentioned in the text. In case help is needed in obtaining these, some of the sources of supply are given below. This is far from a complete list, for the ones given must naturally be those I or my colleagues have used and found good, but there are, of course, other equally excellent supplying firms.

Potclays Limited, Wharf House, Copeland Street, Stoke-on-Trent, Staffs., for clays. We use their red, buff, St. Thomas' body, and Crank mixture—any of them mix well together.

Cromartie Kilns Ltd., Dividy Road, Longton, Stoke-on-Trent, Staffs., for electric kilns. Ours are very reliable and stand constant heavy use. Also for props and shelves.

Alec Tiranti Ltd., 72 Charlotte Street, London, W.1, for banding wheels, plaster and modelling tools.

Podmore & Sons Ltd., Shelton, Stoke-on-Trent, Staffs., for fritted leads.

Geo. Heath & Co. Ltd., Burslem, Stoke-on-Trent, Staffs., for scrapers (called metal palettes).

Potters Equipment Co., 73/77 Britannia Road, London, S.W.6, for very good wheels.

Wengers Ltd., Etruria, Stoke-on-Trent, Staffs., for almost everything! Clays, plaster, sand, grog, all glaze materials, all metal oxides, sieves and brushes, knives and sponges, turning tools and slip trailers, callipers, pestles and mortars, stilts and saddles, cones, wire . . . to mention only a few.